T5-DHG-010

Ahavath Chesed

הגיד לך אדם מה טוב ומה ה׳ דורש ממך כי אם עשות
משפט ואהבת חסד והצנע לכת עם אלקיך.

(מיכה ז, ח)

HE HAS TOLD YOU; O MAN, WHAT IS GOOD, AND
WHAT DOES GOD REQUIRE OF YOU—BUT TO ACT
JUSTLY, TO LOVE CHESED AND TO WALK HUMBLY
WITH YOUR GOD.

(Micah 6.8)

Ahavath Chesed

THE LOVE OF KINDNESS

AS REQUIRED BY GOD

by the Chafetz Chaim

ENGLISH TRANSLATION BY LEONARD OSCHRY

SECOND, REVISED EDITION

FELDHEIM PUBLISHERS

Jerusalem • New York □ 5757 • 1997

©1967, 1976, 1997 by
FELDHEIM PUBLISHERS

FELDHEIM PUBLISHERS
200 Airport Executive Park
Nanuet, NY 10954

POB 35002, Jerusalem, Israel

Printed in Israel

לעילוי נשמת חברי היקר
מרדכי נפתלי הכהן גליקסמן
זכרונו לברכה

TABLE OF CONTENTS

Part III

TRANSLATOR'S PREFACE

The purpose of this translation is not to assist the student who might find certain words or phrases in the Hebrew original somewhat difficult to understand, but to produce, in English, a work faithfully reflecting the train of thought of the sainted Chafetz Chaim of blessed memory. Closer attention had, accordingly, to be paid to clarity, smoothness and readability than to complete verbal accuracy.

The task of the translator was not, on that account, any less demanding. To use the richer English vocabulary with complete abandon would have destroyed the appealing simplicity of the original where every embellishment seems to have been avoided in the interests of absolute honesty and truthfulness. To limit the choice to the very simplest English words, on the other hand, would have rendered the work naive, made it appear irrelevant to the contemporary reader, and nullified its effectiveness. The translator has tried to keep clear of both extremes.

A case in point is the specific mention of money sums in the original. To have left these amounts as they were, would have given the impression that this work only had reference to the East European *Shtetl* of fifty years ago. To give the proper modern equivalents would have required computing the sums in terms of present purchasing power and their relationship to the average person's total earnings — an impossible task. Hence, in almost every instance, specific figures have been omitted. Similar problems. were encountered in the descriptions of commercial activities, and the effort has been made to find the corresponding transaction in modern business.

In spite of all the difficulties, I consider the opportunity to render writings of the Chafetz Chaim into English a rare and inestimable privilege. For who can read the *Ahavath Chesed* without being impelled to enlarge the scope of, and to intensify, his acts of *chesed* in the world? My heartfelt gratitude is extended to Mr. Yaakov Feldheim who granted me this assignment and so allowed me to share, in some modest way, in increasing the observance of this mitzvah among English speaking Jewry. For his act of *chesed*, may he be rewarded with the full measure of blessing recorded in the pages of this book. May the merit of the Chafetz Chaim, *zecher tzaddik livrachah,* protect us all.

Jerusalem, Adar 5726

Leonard Oschry

Note: In preparing this translation, I have not hesitated to make use of the several, superb English versions of Biblical and Rabbinic literature: the Jewish Publication Society translation of the Bible; the Soncino Talmud, Zohar and Midrash; the Yale Judaica series; Avoth de R. Nathan, Pirke de R. Eliezer, etc. To the experts who have rendered these works into Einglish I express my sincere gratitude and unreserved admiration.

GLOSSARY OF UNTRANSLATED TERMS

Acharonim	Later authorities.
Apikoros	Heretic.
Bal Talin	lit. "Shall not remain overnight." The prohibition against withholding the wages of a day laborer.
Beli-Ya'al	"Without yoke." A person who has no restraint.
Bikkur Cholim	The mitzvah of visiting the sick.
Bnei Noach	lit. The descendants of Noah. Non-Jews obliged to observe the seven Noachide commandments.
Beth Din	Court.
Brith Milah	Circumcision.
Chasid	Pious, saintly person.
Chazal	Acronym for *Chachamenu Zichronam Liveracha,* the Sages of blessed memory.
Chesed	Variously translated as "lovingkindness, kindness, benevolence," etc.
Chesed Shel Emeth	The true *chesed,* the chesed extended to the dead, since here no reciprocity can be expected.
Chevra Kadisha	"the Holy Society"—the Jewish Burial society.
Dinar	A silver or gold coin current in Talmudic times.
Gan Eden	The Garden of Eden.
Gemiluth Chesed	The act of bestowing *chesed.*
Gezerah Shavah	lit. "Equal Law"—a hermeneutic principle. The Torah at times uses the same expression in two different contexts to indicate that the rules explicitly stated in the one case apply equally to the other.
Hachnasath Kallah	lit. "Causing the bride to enter" under the bridal canopy. The acts of *chesed* which endow the bride.
Hachnasath Orchim	Reception and care of guests.
Halachah	Jewish legal system of law. (pl. *Halachoth*).
Hashem	God.
Hedkesh	Property dedicated to the Sanctuary.

Heter Iska	Document whereby a loan becomes an investment so that the return is not regarded as usury.
Iska	lit. "Business" or "Occupation".
Kal Vachomer	Reasoning from minor to major, *a fortiori* reasoning.
Kethuvim	Hagiographa.
Kinyan	Symbolic act constituting transfer of ownership or the acceptance of obligation.
Middah	lit. Measure. Virtue or attribute. Character trait.
Minyan	Quorum of ten.
Mitzvah	Torah precept.
Nedivim	lit. "Princes." Here used in a mystic sense.
Nichum Avelim	The mitzvah of comforting mourners.
Peruta	The smallest coin constituting legal tender.
Rasha	Wicked person.
Rebbi	A person's principal Torah teacher.
Ribui	Hermeneutic principle—whereby an extra implication of a Biblical injunction is deduced.
Sefarim	The Holy books used in Torah study.
Shechinah	The Divine Presence.
Shemittah	The Sabbatical year when land is to lie fallow, and at the end of which loan debts are remitted.
Sidrah	The weekly portion of the Torah.
Talmid Chacham	A Torah scholar.
Tanach	Torah, Neviim, Kethuvim—The Bible.
Tanna	Mishnaic Sage.
Techiyath Hamethim	The physical resurrection of the dead.
Tefillah	Prayer.
Teshuvah	Repentance.
Tzaddik	Pious, righteous person.
Tzedakah	Charity or Righteousness.
Yetzer Harah	The human inclination to evil.
Yetzer Hatov	The human inclination to good.

FOREWORD

Praised be *Hashem*, Who is good and does good, and bestows His *chesed* upon all His creatures — as Scripture attests (Ps. 136.25): "He gives food to all flesh, for His *chesed* endures forever" — and especially upon the children of Israel, the people who are near to Him and especially beloved by Him, to the extent that He has referred to them as the "children and portion of God." He commanded them, therefore, to follow in His ways, the paths of *chesed*, compassion and grace. So Scripture confirms (Deut. 10.12): "And now Israel, what does *Hashem* require of you, but to fear Him . . . and to walk in all His ways," and the *Sifrei* explains that the ways of God are: "*Hashem, Hashem*, merciful and gracious God." On the verse: "Everyone that is called by the Name of God shall be saved . . ." it comments further: "How can man possibly be called by the Name of God? — Now, just as God is called compassionate and gracious, you too become compassionate and gracious and dispense gratuitous gifts to all . . ." Not once, but eight times has God admonished us concerning this aspect of conduct (Deut. 8.6; 10.12; 11.22; 13.5 [see *Rashi* there]; 19.9; 26.17; 28.9; 30.16). Moreover, the entire Torah is permeated by this concept, as we shall, God willing, explain fully further on. And He has repeatedly exhorted us through His holy prophets concerning this subject, as Scripture records (Micah 6.8): "He has told you, O man, what is good; and what does God require of you — but to act justly, to love *chesed* and to walk humbly with your God."

15

All these admonitions are for our own benefit alone, as the passage in Deuteronomy (10.12), which we have alluded to, concludes. After first enumerating all these particulars, the verse ends with "that it may be good for you." To the same extent, then, that man accustoms himself to practice the virtues of goodness and kindness throughout all his life, will he enjoy the goodness and abundant *chesed* of the Holy One, blessed be He, in this world and the next. We have found this holy virtue evaluated, in many instances, in the *Kethuvim* and in Rabbinic literature, as being equivalent to Torah study, both in respect of saving man from suffering in this world and the next, and also of making him worthy of receiving all that is good. Now since my space here is limited, I shall confine myself to a few quotations from the *Kethuvim* and Rabbinic literature. As for the rest, we shall, God willing, cite them in the book itself.

Chesed is effective in securing atonement for one's sins, as we find in Scripture (Prov. 16.6): "By *chesed* and truth iniquity is expiated. And *Chazal* have explained (Berachoth 5b): *Chesed* refers to benevolence, as it is stated (Prov. 21.21): "He that pursues righteousness and mercy finds life, righteousness and honor." Truth is Torah, as it is stated (Prov. 23.23): "Buy truth and sell it not." It is recounted in *Avoth de R. Nathan:* Once R. Yochanan b. Zakkai was on his way out of Jerusalem. R. Yehoshua followed him. Seeing the Temple lying in ruins, R. Yehoshua exclaimed: Woe to us, for the place where the transgressions of Israel could be expiated lies in ruins. He (R. Yochanan b. Zakkai) replied: My son, do not grieve. We have another, equally effective form of atonement. What is it? — Acts of *chesed,* since it is written: "For I desire *chesed* and not sacrifice."

Take notice of the power of this holy virtue. It is effective in prolonging human life, as we have found in the case of the sons of Eli. Against them, the decree was pronounced (1 Samuel 2.33): "And all the increase of your house will die young men." Now this decree was reinforced by a Divine oath and could therefore never be

rescinded, as *Chazal* have pointed out. Nevertheless, when the Holy
One, blessed be He, issued this decree against them, He intimated to
them that it could be circumvented by learning Torah and by doing
chesed, and so their lives would be prolonged. For Scripture relates
(Ibid. 3.14): "Therefore I have sworn concerning the house of Eli,
that the iniquity of the house of Eli will never be expiated by sacrifice
or meal offering." Abaye accordingly deduced that the oath could
never be annulled through the medium of sacrificial or meal offerings;
but that it could be obviated by Torah study and *gemiluth chesed*. So
the *Gemarah* (Rosh Hashanah 18a) relates, and adds that both
Abaye and Rava were descendants of the house of Eli. Rava devoted
himself to Torah learning alone and lived to the age of forty. Abaye
was occupied with Torah learning and *gemiluth chesed*, and therefore
lived till sixty. *Gemiluth chesed* avails to save one from the sufferings
of the pre-Messianic era, according to *Chazal* (Sanhedrin 98b). R.
Eliezer's disciples inquired of him: What must a man do to be spared
the birthpangs of the Messiah? He replied: Let him engage in Torah
study and benevolence. This merit will endure for a person through
all succeeding generations, as *Chazal* have declared (*Yalkut
Shim'oni*, Ps. 103.17): *Chesed* stands by man to the end of all
generations, as it is said: "And the kindness of God endures forever
and ever for those that fear Him."

   This mitzvah promotes great peace between us and our Father in
Heaven, as is found in the *Gemara* (Bava Bathra 10a): R. Eliezer b.
Yose declared: All acts of charity and *chesed* performed by Israel in
this world foster great peace and great defence between them and
their Father in Heaven. Whoever seeks to discover how highly this
virtue is regarded by the Torah, will find it placed at the very summit
of human affairs. So the Midrash has it (Ruth Rabba 5.4): Come
and consider how great is the power of those who are charitable and
perform deeds of *chesed*, for they shelter neither in the shadow of the
morning, nor in the shadow of the wings of the earth, nor in the
shadow of the wings of the sun, nor in the shadow of the wings of the

Chayoth or the Cherubim nor in the shadow of eagle's wings; but under whose wings do they shelter? — Under the shadow of Him at Whose word the world was created, as it is said (Ps. 36.8): "How precious is Your *chesed*, O God, and the children of men take refuge in the shadow of Your wings."

Conversely, how deficient is the person lacking the virtues of mercy and *chesed*. He removes himself from the presence of the Holy One, blessed be He, the Source of compassion and grace, and the Torah accordingly designates him as *belia'al*, base. See what *Chazal* have commented (*Yalkut Shim'oni*) on the verse (Deut. 15.9): "Lest there be a base (*belia'al*) thought in your heart, saying: The seventh year, the year of release, is at hand." Beware lest you withhold compassion, for anyone who does is linked to idolatry and removes from himself the Yoke of Heaven, since the term *Belia'al* implies *Beli'ol,* without the Yoke [of Heaven]. Now this verse does not refer only to the withholding of charity, but to refusing to grant free loans as well (as I have found the *Gemara* [Gittin 37a] to indicate; and the same is borne out by the *Sha'are Teshuvah** of R. Yonah, and the *Sefer Hachinuch,* Mitzvah 480). Yet because of our many sins, many people are remiss in this virtue. I therefore sought after the reasons for this neglect and found them to be two. First, people are ignorant of the subject as such; they are unfamiliar with its details, of the instances to which it applies, since the trait of *chesed* is involved in a variety of activites: in acts towards rich as well as towards poor, towards the living and the dead, in kindnesses performed with one's person as well as with one's material resources, as *Chazal* have taught (Sukkah 49b). Every category consists of numerous aspects, and every aspect includes many details. These will be eluciated, God willing, in the chapters that follow. The second cause is that people fail to realize the inherent greatness of this virtue, how mighty is the power it exerts on its exponents, how much

---

*The Gates of Repentance, Feldheim, Jerusalem

good it bestows on them in all their affairs, both in this world and in the world to come, and in saving them on the great day of judgment.

I have accordingly felt myself impelled, by the *chesed* of *Hashem,* may He be blessed, Who extends grace and *chesed* to all His creatures, to set down before all the entire ramifications of this virtue, to the best of my ability, with the help of God, may He be blessed. And I have divided this work into three sections: the first expounding the laws, in their various details, pertaining to the granting of free loans to rich and poor. The laws governing the restoration of pledged articles and the paying of the wages of hired hands on time are also included, as well as other regulations having a practical application. The second section is devoted to elucidating the abundant reward granted, in this world and the next, to those who practice the virtue of *chesed,* and conversely, the dire punishment incurred by those remiss in this virtue. All this has been culled from explicit references in the Babylonian and Palestinian Talmudim and from the relevant Midrashim. Several plans and procedures will be recommended for acquiring, and for removing all hindrances to the acquisition of, this virtue. We shall also explain how one should conduct himself in allocating one tenth or one fifth of his means for charity, as well as much vital information concerning charity. In the third section, the various aspects of *chesed,* such as hospitality to guests, visiting the sick, etc., are discussed.

Now I have entitled the work as a whole AHAVATH CHESED, after the verse: "He has told you, O man, what is good; and what does God require of you — but to act justly, to love *chesed (ahavath chesed)* and to walk humbly with your God." I have also appended a commentary entitled *Nethiv Hachesed**, its name indicating its contents, since it is a "path" guiding the reader to the sources in the Talmud and Codes from which this work has been derived.

---

*In the original Hebrew edition

INTRODUCTION

Rabbi Simlai explained (Sotah 14a): "The Torah begins with an act of kindness (*gemiluth chesed*) and ends with an act of kindness. It begins with *chesed*, as it is written (Gen. 2.21): 'And *Hashem*, God, made for Adam and his wife garments of skins and clothed them.' It ends with *chesed*, as it is written (Deut. 34.6): 'And he (Moses) was buried in the valley in the land of Moab.' " Here *Chazal* have made us aware of the great importance of *gemiluth chesed* by showing that the Torah begins and ends with this topic. In truth, however, these are not the only such passages. Many other sections of the Torah deal with the subject, as we shall, please God, demonstrate. It should, however, first be noted that the scope of this virtue is not limited to free loans, as some believe, but extends through all the good and kind deeds which a person does to another without receiving recompense. One can perform a *chesed* with his possessions: by lending his livestock, utensils, money or the like. This constitutes the kindness done with one's property, and is so called by *Chazal*. One might also extend kindness with his person, this latter category being divisible into two classes: kindness towards the living and kindness towards the dead. Towards the living, one extends *chesed* by welcoming guests into one's house and exerting oneself on their behalf, and by escorting them on their way; by gladdening the groom and his bride; by visiting the sick and by comforting mourners, or by any similar act towards one's neighbor. (All these and similar subjects will be explained in the chapters following.) Then there is the kindness extended towards the dead: taking out the coffin, helping with all necessary for the burial, acting as pall bearer, joining the funeral procession, rising to deliver the eulogy, digging the grave and completing the interment. All such acts are included in the topic of *gemiluth chesed*. (See Sukkah 49b, Rashi there; Rambam: Laws of Mourning, Chap.14 — the sources from which our remarks are derived.) They are included in the positive commandment of (Lev. 19.18): "And you shall love your neighbor as yourself" — meaning that whatever you would want others to do to you, you should do to others.

Now we shall demonstrate for everyone's benefit how the Torah is replete with acts of *chesed*. Every person will then be able to judge for himself how important God, may He be blessed, considers this matter. First of all, on the verse (Gen. 2.22): "And the rib which *Hashem,* God, had taken from the man, made He a woman. And He brought her to the man," *Chazal* have commented (Berachoth 61a): "This teaches that God braided Eve's hair." God also acted as bestman at their wedding (see Gemara there). In the *Sidrah, Noah*, the Torah relates (Gen. 9.21): "And he drank of the wine; and was drunk; and he uncovered within his tent . . . and Ham saw . . . And Shem and Japheth took a garment and laid it upon both their shoulders . . . and they covered the nakedness of their father." (They were not obliged to show this respect; this act is not one of the seven mitzvoth of *Benei Noach*. The sons acted out of *chesed*.) The Torah further quotes the blessing, given by Noah to these sons, which was fulfilled later on. It is mentioned in order to show us the greatness of this virtue. Man must deal benevolently with his fellows and exert himself to the utmost to hide the shame of his fellowmen, just as he would in protecting his own honor. Next, in *Lech Lecha*, the Torah tells of the war of the four kings, and how Abraham strove with all his might, even taking others (Aner, Eshkol and Mamre) with him — all in order to rescue Lot and his possessions from captivity. Now Lot was at fault, as Scripture indicates (Gen. 13.12): "And Lot abode in the cities of the district and moved his tent as far as Sodom." (Here Rashi elucidates [Ibid. 15.14]: "What made this happen to him? — His dwelling in Sodom.") Nevertheless, Abraham extended him the kindness of coming to his rescue. The entire *Sidrah* of *Vayerah* is pervaded by the trait of *chesed*; the very first verse dealing with visiting the sick, the next — the entertainment of guests, then the energetic exertions of our forefather Abraham, all of which were acts of *chesed* (see Bava Metzia 30b; Shabbath 127b). The Torah thereupon informs us of God's love for Abraham, seeing that "he would instruct his sons and his household after him to keep the ways of *Hashem*, to do righteousness and justice," and *chesed* is included in the category of righteousness (*tzedakah*) and even transcends it, as *Chazal* have pointed out. In Abraham's persistent intercession with God, on behalf of the men of Sodom, to bear their iniquity and not destroy them, we see how one should strive to do good to others in every way possible, even to pray for their deliverance, even though they have strayed from the good path. The destruction of Sodom itself teaches the importance of this virtue. The essential wickedness of the inhabitants consisted in their arrogant self-sufficiency, their refusal to help the poor, and their desire to prevent any stranger from entering their territory. So R. Yonah Gerundi has explained in his *Yesod Hateshuvah*. The Torah further relates how Lot exerted himself to the fullest extent to serve the angels, even though he was unaware of their identity. Next we read that (Ibid. 21.33): "Abraham planted a tamarisk" (see Rashi there). Then the *Sidrah* of *Chayei Sarah* is full of the virtue of *chesed*, first of the *chesed* in Abraham's exertions in arranging Sarah's burial and in delivering the eulogy over her. These two acts constitute *gemiluth chesed,* as is evident from the *Gemara*. Next we read a detailed account of the meeting of Isaac and Rebecca, the essential feature being her kindness, as Scripture recounts (Gen. 24.14): "Let the same be she that You have appointed for Your servant, even for Isaac." As Rashi has elaborated, "She is fit for him since she is charitable, and she will be worthy to enter the house of Abraham." Further on (Ibid. 25.9): "And Isaac and Ishmael his sons buried him in the cave of Machpelah." After Abraham's death (Ibid. v. 11) "God blessed Isaac his son," which indicates, according to *Chazal,* that God duly comforted Isaac in his mourning. Then, in *Vayetze* (Gen. 28.20,22), "Jacob vowed a vow saying . . .'And of all that You shall give me, I will surely give a tenth to You.' " Doubtless the tithe was set aside for charitable purposes. Again in *Vayishlach* (Ibid. 35.8,9), God appeared to Jacob when he returned to Padan Aram to pronounce the blessing of the mourners after the death and burial of Deborah, Rebecca's nurse (see Rashi). We are told later (Gen. 35.19) of the burial of Rachel and of the setting of a tombstone on her grave; next of the burial of Isaac (Ibid. v. 29). In *Vayeshev* (Ibid. 37.35): "All his sons and all his daughters rose up to comfort him." Reuben and Judah strove to save Joseph from death and subsequently Jacob commended Judah for this act (Ibid. 49.6): "Judah, you, shall your brothers praise." (Rashi has also pointed out that Tamar was willing to allow herself to be burnt rather than expose the guilty party and put Judah to shame [Gen. 38.25]. This is the kindness which man extends to his fellow.) Later we find (Ibid. 40.14): "Have me in your remembrance when it shall be well with you, and show me kindness . . ." All these types of conduct constitute *gemiluth chesed,* to keep the other person in mind for the purpose of doing good to him, and praise him to those having the power to help him, as we shall, with God's help, explain in the ensuing chapters. Now "Joseph commanded . . .to give them food for the way" (Ibid. 42.25), since this is the proper treatment to accord to departing guests (Sanhedrin 103b). Joseph's dealings with the inhabitants of Egypt (Ibid. 47.13 ff.), his endeavors to preserve their lives and his exertions to sustain them, fall in the category of *chesed,* the worthy relationship of man to his neighbors. What forced Joseph to attempt to acquire the population (as Pharoah's slaves), if not these considerations? Various sections of *Vayechi,* too, speak of *chesed:* the death and burial of Jacob, the weeping over him, the eulogy, the carrying of his bier, and his funeral, all of which are acts of *chesed,* as has been explained. So too, it is written (Ibid. 47.29): "And deal with me in *chesed* and in truth," as Rashi has explained.

The first chapter of Exodus (v. 17) relates: "But the midwives feared God . . . and saved the male children alive." See what *chesed* was performed here! The midwives could have discharged their moral duty both to God and to Pharoah by resigning from their positions. They were concerned, however, that their replacements might, out of fear, carry out Pharoah's designs. Hence they acted charitably towards the daughters of Israel and endangered their own lives for the sake of those women. Furthermore they would provide food and water for the poor women in confinement (see Rashi). Moses (Ibid. 2.11) "went out to his brothers and looked on their burdens." He took their distress to heart, shared in it, and was anxious for them .(Rashi ibid.). This is in accordance with the virtue of *chesed* which obliges one to take account of the sufferings of others, to see whether it is not possible to help them to some extent. "He (Moses) smote the Egyptian" to save the life of the victim (v. 12). Subsequently (v. 17) "Moses stood up and helped the daughters of Jethro," and they related (v. 19): "Moreover he drew water for us and watered the flock." Later, "the officers of the children of Israel were beaten" (Ibid. 5.14). What *chesed* lies here! The officers did not want to drive their workers unmercifully and so took the beatings themselves (see Rashi). Moses took the remains of Joseph with him (Ibid. 14.19), and thus God repaid Joseph for the kindness he had extended in burying his father Jacob (Sotah 9b). Commenting on the verse (Ibid. 15.2): "This is my God and I will glorify Him," Abba Shaul has declared (Sabbath 133b), "Imitate *Hashem.* As He is gracious and merciful, so be you gracious and merciful." (*Veanvehu* is here expounded as *ani vehu,* "I and He.") Moses went out to meet his father-in-law, Jethro (Ibid. 18.7). Here, and in the following verses, the duty of welcoming guests, which is *chesed,* is exemplified. In the verse (Ibid. 20): "And you shall show them the way wherein they shall walk," the "way" is taken by *Chazal* to indicate *gemiluth chesed*. The Ten Commandments announce (Ibid. 20.6) that God shows *chesed* to thousands of generations, and it is necessary for us to follow the example of His virtues. The *Sidrah* of *Mishpatim* (Ibid. 22.24) mentions the duty of "lending money to My people" and the regulations governing the restoration of a pledge (Ibid. v. 11) which also stem from the virtue of benevolence, as is explained in Deuteronomy (24.13). Many topics are discussed in the *Sidrah* of *Behar* (Lev. Chap. 25), all of them aspects of *chesed*, such as: redeeming relatives from slavery and "Your brother shall live with you."

I thereupon concluded that there is no end, indeed, to the *chesed* mentioned in the Torah. So many positive and negative commandments emanate from His virtue of *chesed*, may He be blessed. There are *leket, shikhchah, peah* (leaving the gleanings, forgotten sheaves and the corners of the harvested field for the poor); the tithe of the poor and *shemittah*, which is not only "a sabbatical year to God," but also has this aspect (Exod. 23.11): "But the seventh year you shall let it rest and lie fallow, that the poor of your people may eat with you." Then there is the commandment to return lost property — the Torah admonishes us to guard the possessions of a fellow Jew. Even if the article in question is only worth a *perutah*, one must take the trouble to restore it to its rightful owner. Helping to load and unload (Exod. 23.5) and many other such mitzvoth are all included in this category and all emanate from God's goodness and kindness. He has, therefore, also commanded us to come to the aid of our fellow man in every way possible. Hence I have refrained from enumerating all the other instances.

From what has been cited above, the intelligent reader will be able to appreciate that the holy virtue of *chesed* is of such supreme importance that the entire Torah is pervaded by it. How tenaciously should one cling to this holy trait and not weaken his hold of it all the days of his life on earth! In this connection, the Torah states (Deut. 19.9): "to walk in His ways all the days" — meaning that one should not be satisfied with the occasional performance of an act of *chesed* once a month or once a week, as we shall explain (Part II, Chap. 12). It is also necessary to be familiar with the laws governing the exercise of this virtue — all the details pertaining to the matters we have mentioned in the beginning of this introduction. First of all, however, the topic of free loans will be taken up since, for it, there is a specific, explicit Scriptural command, "If you will lend money to My people." We shall explain this further on. Before we proceed to the actual laws as such, however, we shall give a general review of the many negative commandments transgressed by one who habitually acts the miser and abstains from deeds of *chesed*:

(1) It is written in the Torah (Deut. 15.9): "Beware lest there be a base thought in your heart saying: 'The seventh year, the year of release, is at hand.'" The *Sifrei* here remarks that "Beware" and "lest" each introduce a negative commandment. Hence two negative commandments order us not to abstain from lending to our neighbor in need, for fear of the *shemittah* ordinance remitting debts. Scripture has termed the person guilty of such conduct a *beliya'al*, a base person; and certainly when a person has the capacity to do good to another and he does not stand to lose his money, the sin of "closing his fist" against lending to his neighbor is all the greater.

(2) Occasionally, by refraining from doing a favor, one transgresses the negative commandment of "You shall not take vengeance." For instance, he had previously asked a favor of someone, either a loan of money or the like, and the other person had failed to help him. Now that other person comes to him for a favor and he gains his revenge, repaying that person by refusing to help. In this case, by refraining from doing a favor, the person transgresses the commandment (Lev. 19.18), "You shall not take vengeance." If, through his hatred of that person, he spreads the report in the city that the other

person is not reliable, thereby discouraging others from granting the loan that person requires, he transgresses all the more. In addition to violating the two prohibitions against taking revenge and bearing a grudge, he transgresses the commandment forbidding slander (*leshon hara'*), since here he attacks the person's very life. (See *Chafetz Chayim*, Chap. 5. Par. 5, and at the end of the book in the *Be'ar Mayim Chayim* s.s.2, second illustration.) Furthermore, even if he had helped that other person, but rebuked him by saying: "I am not like you; you did not help me," he violates the prohibition (Lev. 19.18): "You shall bear no grudge," since he has shown here that he still harbors the hate in his heart. He should erase his ill-feeling and lend with a perfect heart, reflecting that all the affairs of this world are vain and worthless, not important enough to arouse the desire for revenge and grudges. (See below Chap. 4, Par. 4 and 5.)

(3) If the person who asks for a loan is liable to be in danger if his request is refused, if he needs the money to prevent robbers attacking him, then whoever refuses to help in such a case would violate the additional prohibition of (Lev. 19.16): "Neither shall you stand idly by the blood of your neighbor." Here we have been warned against remaining indifferent to our friend when his life is in danger and we have the means to save him in one way or another. Furthermore according to the *Mechilta* (cited by the Rambam in his *Sefer Hamitzvoth* No. 297), this prohibition also applies to the case where one is aware of something which might cause loss to his neighbor and he is able to help prevent it. If he fails to help, he commits the transgression. This applies to our case too. If one knows that his friend, rich or poor, is liable to incur a substantial loss (as happens nowadays when a loan falls due, as is well known), and by a loan given now he can save his friend, then if he fails to help he violates this prohibition.

Now we shall enumerate the positive commandments which the

niggardly person, who refrains from doing *chesed*, is liable to transgress:

(1)   He violates the command of the Torah (Deut. 28.9): "And you shall walk in His ways." We are obliged by this overall injunction to follow the attributes of God, all of which consist in doing good to others, as *Chazal* have laid down (Sotah 14a): "As He is merciful, so you be merciful; as He is gracious, so you be gracious," and so in reference to the other virtues as well. The Rambam has quoted the entire passage in his *Sefer Hamitzvoth* (No. 8). (The mitzvah of walking in the ways of *Hashem* is repeated eight times in Deuteronomy alone, as explained in the foreword.) Whoever refrains from doing good to his fellow man, without just cause, transgresses this positive commandment which God has many times ordered us to obey.

(2)   One further violates the specific Scriptural commandment to perform acts of *chesed* (Exod. 18.20): "And you shall show them the way wherein they must walk," where "the way" is taken by *Chazal* (Bava Kamma 99b; Bava Metzia 30b) to indicate *chesed*. The inference is derived from the definite article, *the*, which has no specific reference and must therefore signify the well-trodden path along which our forefather, Abraham, walked, and whose entire life was bound up with the virtue of *chesed*, as everyone knows. This admonition includes all the types of kindness arising in personal relationships, also the *gemiluth chesed* extended with one's person: visiting the sick, burying the dead, etc., as is explained in the *Gemarah* (Ibid.). Nor is the *gemiluth chesed* performed with one's possessions, by any means, excluded from this rule.

(3)   If a poor man has become financially unstable, and a loan might strengthen his position, stave off ruin and save him from dependence on charity, then the person who refuses to give such a

loan transgresses another commandment of the Torah (Lev. 25.35):
"And if your brother be waxen poor and his means fail with you,
you shall strengthen him, [even if he is] a stranger and a settler; he
shall live with you." Scripture admonishes again (v. 36): "And your
brother shall live with you." We have accordingly been obliged by
this positive commandment to strengthen the hand of our brother
who has become poor, to grant him a gift or loan, to enter into
partnership with him, or else to provide him with employment, so
that he might be self-supporting, and not suffer financial ruin,
becoming dependent on charity. Whoever abstains from providing
the proper succor, violates this positive mitzvah.

(4)   Above all, the one refusing aid transgresses the specific commandment of the Torah regarding loans themselves, the Scriptural
passage: "If you will lend money to My people, the poor that is with
you." *Chazal* have it by tradition that this "if" does not denote an
option, but a definite obligation, one we have been commanded to
obey — to lend money to our brothers in their time of need. The commandment is repeated in *Re-eh* (Deut. 15.8): "You shall surely lend
to him." This applies to loans. (The Torah uses the word "if" since
this is the condition upon which the end of the sentence depends,
"You shall not be to him a creditor" — since this injunction only applies when the borrower is Jewish and not a Gentile. See too what I
have written in this connection in the *Nethiv Hachesed*, Chap. I, subsection 2, in the Hebrew edition of this work.) The details of these
laws will be explained in the forthcoming chapters, please God.

We have now enumerated the many commandments, negative and
positive, transgressed by the niggardly, the person lacking in *chesed*.
Now although all these mitzvoth, negative and positive, seldom occur all together in a single, given instance, as is obvious to the careful
reader, nevertheless a person who is accustomed to act according to
bad characteristic traits will transgress them all in the course of time.
Hence anyone concerned for his soul will carefully guard against ac-

quiring this evil trait. He will follow the ways of *Hashem*, may He be blessed, Who is good and Who does good, as Scripture enjoins us "to walk in all His ways." For this merit God's blessing will be vouchsafed him, and in him will the Scriptural dictum be fulfilled (Isa. 3.10): "Say of the righteous that it shall be well with him, for they shall eat the fruits of their doing."

And now we shall, with God's help, begin to elucidate all the ramifications and details of the positive commandment of giving free loans.

I

LAWS OF LOANS, PLEDGES AND WAGES

1

THE POSITIVE COMMANDMENT
"IF YOU WILL LEND MONEY TO MY PEOPLE"

(1)   It is a positive commandment of the Torah to lend to the poor among our brothers, as it is said (Exod. 22.24): "If you will lend money to My people, to the poor that is with you . . ." The *Mechilta* observes that all "if"'s in the Torah express an option, except three, which introduce an obligation, and this is one of the three. The proof lies in the statement [Deut. 15.8] "You shall surely lend to him," which is expressed as an imperative. This mitzvah is superior to charity, since here the poor is not put to shame by accepting gifts, and since here also his hand is strengthened; he is supported and protected from financial ruin. By such an act, the lender fulfills the mitzvah of the Torah (Lev. 25.35): "And if your brother be waxen poor and his hand fail with you, you shall uphold him," so that he should not be ruined and become dependent on charity. This commandment is also fulfilled by giving loans to the rich for a certain period, when they are pressed for money, since *chesed* may be done both to rich and poor. The only difference is that the poor take priority, and for that reason Scripture had made explicit mention of the poor in its reference to the mitzvah. If Scripture had not made us aware of our obligation, we would prefer to lend to the rich only, since one is likely to receive many favors in return, and, moreover, the rich person is a more reliable risk.

(2)   Know, too, that this mitzvah does not only cover loans of
money, but applies equally to loans of utensils and other articles. All
such acts emanate from the virtue of *chesed*, which God desires us to
embody, as it is said (Micah 7.18): "For He delights in *chesed*." And
chesed includes any act by which one person can confer benefit on
another. (We shall, please God, elucidate this assertion in Part III by
reference to Scriptural verses and Rabbinic dicta). Money loans,
however, constitute the greater mitzvah, since Scripture contains a
separate, explicit reference to them. (*Chazal* have declared that if
one is persistently requested to lend utensils to his neighbor, and he
lies, denying that he has them, plagues attack his house by way of
punishment; he is then forced to remove all his possessions from his
house and his falsehood is publicly exposed.)

(3)   What has been said so far applies to a rich person. When a
poor person, however, approaches someone for the use of some
utensil or other article, the law places a heavy obligation on the
person approached, since the applicant may not have the means to
purchase this item. (See Part II, Chap. 20, where we have dealt with
the subject at length.) It is our intention, after all, to elaborate
somewhat on this type of *chesed*, to describe how every person is to
behave in such matters, but since money loans, which are also included in the virtue of *chesed*, are the most frequently encountered of
all types, and since they are governed by a separate, positive mitzvah, we shall devote our attention to this aspect, and the intelligent
reader will be able to draw the proper conclusions regarding the
other types of *chesed*.

(4)   Because of my own limitations, I have not been able to discover any mention, by *Chazal*, of a fixed measure for loans. Nor can
any conclusions be drawn from the laws of charity. There the maximum limit is one fifth of one's possessions, because this is an outright gift. Here, however, the lender regains possession of his money.

Nor can the opposite inference be drawn, viz. that the Torah has ordered one to allocate all his idle capital to money loans, since the owner might find the opportunity to make some profitable investment, advantageous to his household, and then he would not have the money available. (See Bava Metzia 42a: "And R. Yitzchak said . . ." Rashi s.v. *Matzui*.) The logical approach would be that each person should act in accordance with his means, and should extend whatever favor he can to his friend. I have found, with God's help, that the *Sefer Hachinuch*, too, has followed this principle. (See Part II, Chap. 18. There we have explained how each person may discharge his moral obligation.)

(5)   It may further be inferred from the *Sefer Hachinuch* that the amount of the loan will depend on the needs of the borrower, as long as the lender can afford such an amount. Indeed this is stated explicitly in a passage of the Torah (*Re-eh*, Deut. 15.8): "You shall surely lend him (*ta'avitenu* signifying lending, according to · *Chazal*), and the verse concludes with "sufficient for his needs."

(6)   For what period must the loan be granted? Here, too, the logical answer is that this depends on what each person is able to afford. The lender is not obliged to extend the loan longer than for a day or two, if he cannot. The converse holds true as well. If the lender can afford to, it seems that he is obliged to grant the loan for more than thirty days, if the borrower requires the amount for a longer period.

(7)   No limitation has been set for the number (even if it reaches 100) of times the loans are to be granted. The person approached should not resent the inconvenience and be annoyed by the borrower pestering him so many times, coming to borrow or to repay, just as one never resents the constant visits to one's store of a regular customer from whom one profits. The lender should remember that

each time he lends, he is fulfilling a positive commandment of the Torah. God's blessing will rest on him, since Scripture has given its assurance in the similar case of charity (Ibid. v. 10): "Give — give to him (the repetition implying over and over again, even a hundred times [Rashi], and your heart shall not be grieved; because for this thing, *Hashem,* your God, will bless you in all your work ..."

(8)   The Torah obligation to lend to one's fellow man covers both cases: where a security pledge is given, and also where no pledge is given, the borrower himself being sufficiently reliable. Yet, if one does extend the loan without taking any pledge, the lender should nevertheless hand over the money in the presence of witnesses or take a note from the borrower, or at least obtain his signature. The borrower might be trustworthy; but he might forget and later on deny ever having taken the loan.

(9)   If one knows that the applicant for the loan has bad traits and is careless with other people's money, and someone lending to this person would stand to lose his money, since there will be nothing left from which to collect, it is better not to lend without taking a pledge, than to lend and to be compelled to keep dunning the debtor for repayment, since the creditor will thereby transgress the prohibition (Ibid. 15.2): "He shall not exact it of his neighbor." So the ruling is recorded in *Choshen Mishpat* (Chap. 97, Par. 4, q.v. — "Such a borrower is also called a *rasha*' ") (See Part II, Chap. 24).

(10)   Shimon approached Reuven and said: "Lend me a sum of money. I cannot, however, repay in one lump sum, only little by little." In this case the law does not require Reuven to grant the loan. It would be right to extend this loan, however, out of friendship and brotherhood.

(11)   Once a person has agreed to lend a sum of money to a fellow Jew, he must take all precautions not to break his word, since his

consent here is as binding as in any other undertaking to perform a mitzvah. *Yoreh Deah* has ruled (Chap. 213, Par. 2) that in such cases it is forbidden to retract. (In the *Nethiv Hachesed* it is stated that giving a long-term loan to a rich person is not considered a mitzvah. Hence, one's word is not considered to be in the nature of a vow. Nevertheless, where the person approached is aware that the rich man relies on him, it is well for him to take care that he not be classed as one unworthy of trust. Again, if a person has set aside, or has expressly vowed, a sum of money for free loans, he is forbidden to retract.)

(12) Know that the mitzvah does not apply where the person approached has no ready cash. He is not obliged to borrow in order to give loans, even though the applicant can furnish a pledge or is completely reliable. For him to borrow would be a virtuous act of *chesed*, only. If his money was lent out, and the due date for its repayment had passed, some authorities consider him as having the money available. Hence, he is obliged to go and secure the return of his money and to lend it to the present applicant. The obligation would be even greater where his money had been deposited with a third party. In this case all authorities agree that this person cannot release himself from his obligation just because his money is not in his domain. The law always regards a deposit as being in the owner's possession, irrespective of its location. He is therefore obliged by law to obtain the return of his money and grant the loan. If he is unwilling to make the effort, the law obliges him to borrow from some other source to lend to this applicant. His duty is even greater where he has the money at hand, but is reluctant to grant the loan because of the family quarrels such an act would arouse. He must then borrow from another source, since he really does have the money, and the duty to perform the mitzvah devolves on him (see Chap. 2).

(13) Today, money, unless packaged and sealed, is regarded as having no identity and may be used by the trustee, since we are all

considered today as shopkeepers and moneychangers were in times gone by. (See *Choshen Mishpat*, Chap. 292, Par. 7; *acharonim* ibid.) Nevertheless, one has no right to lend out money deposited with him without the express consent of the depositor, unless the borrower will agree to repay on demand.

(14) Where many applicants for loans approched him, one needing a larger sum, and each of the others requiring a small amount, and by lending to the first applicant he would have none left for the others, then the lending of small amounts to the many is preferable to the lending of a large sum to a single borrower. Each individual loan constitutes a fulfillment of a positive mitzvah, and the *Tanna* has already declared (Avoth 3.15): "All depends on the number of acts." (See Rambam: Mishnah Commentary, ad loc.). If, however, the applicant for the larger sum would thereby be saved from complete financial ruin, he might take priority over the others, since here an additional mitzvah is involved, viz. (Lev. 25.35): "And if your brother be waxen poor and his means fail with you, you shall uphold him." In assisting the many, the mitzvah of giving loans, alone, is fulfilled.

2

WHO ARE OBLIGED BY LAW TO LEND

(1)   All Jews are obliged, in accordance with their means, to give free loans whether they be man or woman, rich or poor (lending to one in poorer circumstances than he). The Torah has not assigned any fixed amounts for loans, and the mitzvah is similar to *tzedakah*, to which all Israel are obliged, as the *Gemara* and *Yoreh Deah* (Chap. 248, Par. 1) point out.

(2)   When does the obligation devolve on a woman? — When she has no husband. If she has a husband, she does not have the right to lend out his money without his consent, even if she engages in business at home, unless the amount is so small that people would not normally object, or else it is not her husband's nature to object. This restriction only applies to loans of money. The wife is permitted, however, to lend out the household utensils, which neighbors are accustomed to allow each other to use, without his knowledge. Where the wife objects to her husband making *gemiluth chesed* loans and quarrels with him over them, the law does not require him to pay heed to her, since the money is his. Nevertheless, it is better for him to dispense the loans secretly to avoid arguments and disputes. The woman who protests against her husband fulfilling the mitzvah of *gemiluth chesed*, or other mitzvoth, commits a transgression and is destined to be called to account. On the other hand, if she encourages him to perform mitzvoth, she will receive her due merit.

(3)   One whose occupation is to lend money (to non-Jews on interest and to Jews with the *heter iska*) is still obliged to grant free loans to the poor in accordance with his ability. (See below Chap. 5, Par. 3; Chap. 6, Par. 9; Part II, Chap. 8.)

(4)   If the request is addressed to a person engaged in full time Torah study, and the mitzvah cannot be fulfilled by others, he is obliged to interrupt his studies and grant the loan. It makes no difference in this case whether the others are unable or unwilling to do the favor. (This is similar to the case mentioned in the *Chochmath Adam* quoted from the *Radvaz*, where a poor man's rich relatives refused to support him, and the obligation therefore devolved on the rest of the community.)

(5)   For many reasons, this mitzvah does not oblige a storekeeper to extend credit to his customers. Firstly, his main source of income is the selling of his wares. He reinvests the proceeds in inventory. If he grants credit, he will not have the wherewithal to replenish his stocks. Moreover, customer credit does not belong in the category of loans, as is proved by the *Mishnah* (Shevi'ith Chap. 10). Hence, to extend credit is not included in this mitzvah. Nevertheless, it appears that if a poor customer requests the storekeeper to supply him with a few items for his immediate needs, the storekeeper is not exempt from this obligation, if he is able to comply with the request. Even though such an act is not included in the positive mitzvah of: "If you will lend money to My people," it is surely not excluded from the admonition: "If your brother be waxen poor and his means fail with you, you shall uphold him." *Chazal* have said: "Uphold him before he falls and becomes dependent on charity."

3

TO WHOM GEMILUTH CHESED MUST BE EXTENDED

(1) *Gemiluth chesed* loans are to be extended to all: man or woman, rich or poor, adults or minors (through their guardian and the like, to prevent the money being lost. *Gemiluth chesed* with one's person is to be extended to the minor directly). Scripture has stated: "If you will lend money to My people." Whoever is included in the term "My people" is entitled by law to benefit from *gemiluth chesed*, and the list of priorities is set down in Chaps. 4 and 5.

(2) Even though the applicant is known as the habitual transgressor, because of lack of restraint, of a mitzvah of the Torah, he is still within the fold of Israel, since anyone who subscribes to the thirteen cardinal principles of our faith is classed as a *Yisrael*. (This excludes the *apikoros*, as is explained in the *Choshen Mishpat*, ibid.) The Torah mitzvah requires that one have compassion on such a person and extend *chesed* to him in his time of need. Where one knows, however, that the money will be used for some unlawful purpose, it is certainly forbidden to give to him. One doing so is called an abettor of transgressors.

(3) Know that one publicly desecrating the Sabbath is excluded from the community of *Yisrael* and is considered a non-Jew. An informer is also excluded from the mitzvah of brotherhood. He is not to receive *gemiluth chesed*. All the above applies where the guilty

person has not repented. If he has, then nothing stands in the way of *teshuvah*. The person is disqualified only where he is definitely known to be, or is commonly regarded as, guilty of this evil conduct. Mere suspicion, however, does not exclude him from brotherly consideration. (See *Sefer Chafetz Chaim*, Laws Prohibiting *Leshon Hara'*, Chap. 6, the note on Par. 10.)

4

HATED PERSONS ARE NOT EXCLUDED:
THE PROHIBITION AGAINST TAKING REVENGE

(1)   The law to extend *chesed*, as ordained by the Torah, makes no distinction between friend and foe — even in giving one hundred times. The Torah has made this explicit in the mitzvah of restoring lost property (Exod. 23.4): "If you meet your enemy's ox or his ass going astray, you shall surely bring it back to him again." The mitzvah of "unloading" makes the same stipulation (Ibid. v. 5): "If you see the ass of him that hates you lying under its burden, you shall not forbear to pass by him. You shall surely release it with him." Here the *Gemara* (Bava Metzia 31a) adds that one is obliged to help even a hundred times.

(2)   There is no question of one's obligation where the resentment is not justified, as when the other person had refused him a favor, since his refusal on such grounds would not only violate the positive commandment of *chesed* but would also be a transgression of the Torah's prohibition against taking vengeance or bearing a grudge, as is explained below in Par. 4. Yet even if the Torah requires him to, and he does hate a person, as where he knew of that person's transgression of the law against forbidden unions, etc., where no one is ignorant of the law, nevertheless he is obliged to help that person when in need, since that person subscribes to the cardinal principles of our faith. (See above, Chap. 3.)

(3) There is, however, one distinction. If the one against whom he harbors an unjustified hatred and a friend both requested the same favor, and he is unable to help both, he is duty bound to help the one he hates, so as to overcome his prejudice. Where the Torah requires him to hate a person, as defined above, and that person and another approached him at the same time, it is the greater mitzvah to help a worthy person rather than one guilty of improper conduct.

(4) The Torah prohibition (Lev. 19.18): "You shall not take revenge or bear any grudge against the children of your people," is elucidated in the *Baraitha* (Yoma 23a): "What is revenge? — If one says to another: Lend me your sickle. He replies, No. The next day the latter says to the former: Lend me your hatchet. He retorts: I am not going to lend it to you, because you refused to lend me your sickle. This is taking revenge. What is bearing a grudge? — If one to another: Lend me your sickle. He says, No. The next day he says to him: Lend me your hatchet. He replies: Here it is. I am not like you. You refused to lend to me. This constitutes bearing a grudge." By using these examples the *Gemara* intended to convey that the prohibition against taking revenge or bearing a grudge applies even in minor matters like these. It applies with even greater force to important things, like refusing to help in matters affecting a person's livelihood. The *Sifra* emphasizes: "*How far* does the prohibition against revenge extend? He said: Lend me your sickle ... *How far* does the bearing of a grudge extend? He said: Lend me your sickle, and the other did not lend it to him ..." R. Eliezer of Metz has similarly recorded in his work (*Yerei'im* 41) that not only household utensils (since utensils are not expressly mentioned in the Torah), but any other property not included in that category are affected as well. "We have learned that Jews are prohibited from withholding charity or refusing free loans with their property, on the grounds that the person requesting them had previously refused the other's request,

since this would constitute revenge. They are also prohibited ...
since this would constitute bearing a grudge."

(5)   Know, too, that all the earlier authorities (*Rishonim*) concur
that the prohibition against taking revenge is transgressed even
where the person did not expressly declare, "I will not lend you ..."
As long as he knows in his heart that this is the motive behind his
refusal, he commits the violation. The same applies to bearing a
grudge. The prohibition is not only transgressed by uttering the
remark, but by bearing the grudge inwardly. One is required to erase
such feelings from his heart. (See *Chafetz Chaim*, Introduction, Par.
9 and 10, where the laws against taking revenge and bearing grudges
have been elaborated.)

5

THE ORDER OF PRIORITY IN LOANS

(1) If both a Jew and non-Jew had applied for loans and both offer pledges or equal security, preference must be given to the Jew, since Scripture states: "If you will lend money to *My people*." As *Chazal* have stated (Bava Metzia 71a): "My nation comes first."

(2) Even if the non-Jew is willing to pay interest, while the Jew desires a free loan, preference must be given to the Jew. It makes no difference whether the borrower is rich or poor, since the money is needed for his livelihood. If the Jewish borrower intends to lend out this money, he, nevertheless, takes precedence.

(3) If someone's main income is derived from lending out money to non-Jews on interest, his own needs come first. Where, however, an indigent person requests a loan of him in order to buy food, then the indigent takes precedence. This is recorded in the *Sefer Agudah* (See Chap. 6, Par. 9, where we have shown how this law affects rich and poor.)

(4) The law of granting a Jew priority over a non-Jew only applies where the two make their requests simultaneously. If the non-Jew came first on his own, it is permissible to lend him the money at interest (especially according to the *Rambam*, who considers this act the fulfillment of a positive commandment), unless the lender knows for sure that a Jew will approach him soon afterwards. In that event he should refrain from granting the loan to the non-Jew.

46

(5)   Know that in this law of preferring the free loan to a Jew to the loan at interest to a non-Jew, the authorities hold conflicting opinions. Some assert that even if the lender would derive a substantial return from the loan to the non-Jew, the Torah still obliges him to give the free loan to the Jew, as long as the amount is within his means. He incurs no loss in lending to the Jew, since his money will be restored to him. He only fails to earn the profit for the period of the loan. Moreover, his livelihood is not affected, as was explained above. Others, however, rule that the priority is only in force where the return is small. Where the profits are large, he is not required to forego them. This opinion seems evident to some extent in a Responsum of the *Rema* (No. 10).

(6)   Be it noted further, that the same consideration applies to buying and selling. Where a Jew has something to sell, and both a Jew and a non-Jew wish to buy it, he should sell to the Jew, and the same preference is followed in buying. So Scripture ordains (Lev. 25.14): "And if you sell ought to your neighbor, or buy from your neighbor's hand." Here the *Sifra* elucidates: "If you sell, sell to your neighbor, the Israelite. And if you buy, buy from your neighbor, the Israelite." Obviously, the same rule applies to the renting of an article or tool. It is better to rent from a Jew if the renter will derive equal benefit from either one.

(7)   Even if the non-Jew is willing to pay somewhat more, nevertheless, it is preferable to sell to the Jew for less. The same principle applies to buying. It is better to pay the Jewish seller a slightly higher price (*Rema* in the above-mentioned Responsum).

(8)   If a Jew wishes to borrow, and a non-Jew to hire, the same article, then even if the latter only wishes to pay a small sum for its use, there is no obligation to give preference to the Jew. This is different from the law of loans. There one is obliged to lend to a Jew

without return even if this would entail forfeiting the interest offered by the non-Jew, firstly because loans are governed by the specific positive mitzvah of "If you will lend money to My people" and the "if" according to *Chazal* here introduces an obligation. Secondly, the money loaned will eventually be restored. This is not so with respect to articles, since these depreciate through use. However, if the borrower is poor and needs the article for his livelihood, then the owner is obliged to lend it to him in obedience to the positive commandment of "And if your brother be waxen poor . . . and you shall uphold him and your brother shall live with you."

(9)   In obtaining loans, it seems to me, a man takes preference over a woman, if neither is poor; and certainly where the man is poor but not the woman. When both are poor, however, the woman comes first, unless the man is related to the lender, since then he would, logically, take preference, as we have written in the following chapter. If mortal danger might result from withholding a loan, the man will take preference since he is obliged to perform all the mitz- voth, while the woman is exempt from positive commandments which have to be performed at a set time.

6

OTHER LAWS OF PRIORITY

(1) A poor and a rich man approached a person for a loan. The lender is unable to give to both. If the poor man is trustworthy or can furnish a pledge, he has preference, since Scripture ordains: "If you will lend money to My people, to *the poor* that is with you." And *Chazal* have stated: "Rich and poor — the poor comes first." Even if the rich is a fellow townsman and is related to the lender, while the poor is from another city and is not related, the poor takes preference. Where both applicants are poor, and the one requires the money for food, the other for clothing, the loan should be given to the one requiring food, since his situation is the more pressing. (A deduction from *Yoreh Deah*, Chap. 251, Par. 7. There the reference is to charity, and the inference is drawn to loans.)

(2) If the two applicants are poor, and one is a relative or a fellow townsman, he takes priority, since it is written: "The poor that is *with you.*" A relative or fellow townsman is considered "with you." It is a mitzvah to give him preference. (See *Yoreh Deah*, Chap. 251, Par. 3. There the *Rema* notes that one's neighbors take priority over the rest of the city.) The "poor of the city" are all who have resided there for at least twelve months. If a person had purchased a dwelling, or his intention was to take up permanent residence, he is immediately regarded as a member of the city.

(3) If one of the applicants is his relative, but lives in another city, while the other lives in the same city as he, but is not related to

him, then the relative takes priority, since "with you" applies more readily to the relative. If the relative is able to procure the loan from others without difficulty, and the other applicant cannot, then apparently it seems that the townsman will take precedence over the relative.

(4) Who is termed a relative in this context? — The same criterion applies here, obviously, as in the case of charity (*Yoreh Deah*, Chap. 251, Par. 3; the same is evident from the *Sefer Me'iroth Enayim, Choshen Mishpat*, Chap. 93). Hence, in loans, consideration is given to parents before one's own children, one's children before one's brother, one's paternal brother before his maternal brother, his brother before other relatives.

(5) Similarly, be it noted, if two rich people approached him, and one of them is his relative, then the relative comes first.

(6) If several people, all either rich or poor, made requests for loans simultaneously, and the lender is unable to give to all of them, then the Priest comes before the Levite, the Levite before an ordinary Jew, and the ordinary Jew before one of illegitimate birth. This order is followed where all are equally learned in Torah. If the illegitimate person was a *Talmid Chacham*, however, he takes precedence. Even where the sage requires the sum for clothes and the unlearned for food, the sage has preference. The wife of a *Talmid Chacham* assumes his status. The order of precedence corresponds to the level of Torah learning.

(7) If one of the applicants was his main "*rebbi*", the teacher from whom he had acquired most of his Torah learning, or his father, then they precede everyone else, even a *Talmid Chacham*. In his novellae, R. Akiva Eger has ruled that the rest of one's relatives, too, take precedence over a *Talmid Chacham*.

(8)   If his father and his "rebbi" wish to borrow from him, the "rebbi" has priority over the father, since the "rebbi" brings him to the world to come, while his father only gives him life in this world. If his father were as learned as his "rebbi", then the father takes priority. This order only applies where the "rebbi" is not paid tuition. Where the father hires the instructor, the father comes first.

(9)   Know that the precedence given to the poor as against the rich, mentioned above (as well as the priority sequence set down in this chapter), is only in force where both apply for free loans. If the rich required the loan for an investment, and the lender would lose his share of the profits by giving the money to the poor without charge, and he cannot afford this loss, he is not obliged to give the money as a free loan to the poor. (See Chapter 1 where we have cited the opinion of the *Chinuch* that the mitzvah of *gemiluth chesed* loans depends on each person's circumstances.) In this connection, *Chazal* (Bava Metzia 33a) have stated that (Deut. 15.4) "Howbeit, there shall be no needy among you" signifies that "your" needs come first. One should, however, most carefully consider whether he really is unable to afford the loan, for the evil inclination always entices one to believe that one does not have the means. Now, if one really can afford the loan, yet he closes his fist and refuses to do *chesed* fearing that he might thereby become impoverished, his evil streak will eventually bring him, God forbid, to poverty. So *Chazal* have declared (Bava Metzia 32a): "Whoever [overly] considers his own needs first, will come to be in need." This criterion of whether he really has the means applies not only to the case mentioned above, but also where he wants to invest the money in business and a poor man desires to borrow that sum as a free loan (see Part II, Chap. 10).

(10)   Know also that our ruling, that the poor precedes the rich, not only applies to where the poor is really indigent, but also to where one has not yet become poor, only hard pressed in business,

and is in danger of being ruined if the loan is denied to him. Apparently, in this case, too, the law requires that priority be given to him, since here the commandment, "And his means fail with you; you shall uphold him," will also be fulfilled.

(11)   If one knows for sure that his poor relative will soon apply to him for a loan, he may, on these grounds, deny a loan at this time to another poor person who is not his relative. If there is a mere possibility that his relative will approach him, he cannot exempt himself for this reason. (See *Nethiv Hachesed* in the Hebrew edition.)

(12)   Two people requested loans, one of them having rich relatives capable of helping him, and the other not having any. It is better here to lend to the applicant not having rich relatives. If the former protests that his own relatives do not wish to help him, then both have equal rights.

(13)   Where someone entrusted money to a third party to dispense free loans, the relatives of the owner receive no priority over other applicants (even less do the relatives of the Loan Fund treasurer have any preferential rights). Once the owner has transferred his money for this mitzvah to a third party, the transferee assumes the function of a charity treasurer who acquires the money on behalf of all the inhabitants of the city.

(14)   The above order of priority not only applies to loans of cash and commodities (which are also in the same category) but to any other favor, as for instance in hiring for gainful employment, etc.

7

LAWS OF PLEDGES

(1)   If one person lent money to another to be repaid on a certain date, and the lender took no pledge, and the debt fell due and the debtor was delinquent, then the lender is forbidden to enter the borrower's house and seize a pledge. The Torah has warned (Deut. 24.10): "When you lend your neighbor any manner of loan, you shall not go into his house to fetch his pledge." Whether the lender snatched the pledge by force or the borrower stood silently by without protesting, or else was away from his home at the time, the lender violates a negative commandment, since he took the pledge on his own. Even if he keeps pestering there till the debtor finally gives him the pledge of his own volition, the transgression is committed. Instead, the creditor must remain outside and the debtor must bring the pledge to him. So Scripture orders (Ibid. v. 11): "You shall stand without, and the man to whom you lend shall bring forth the pledge without unto you." Not only to enter the debtor's house, but even to encounter him in the street and there to seize a pledge from him by force, is prohibited, unless the borrower gives the pledge of his own volition.

(2)   The messenger of the Rabbinical court is also prohibited from entering the borrower's house to take a pledge, since it is written: "You shall stand without and the man" and *Chazal* take "man" here to refer also to the messenger of the court. The word is understood as pertaining to the preceding sentence, thus meaning that the

53

messenger of the *Beth Din*, too, shall stand outside. The messenger would be permitted, however, to seize the pledge from the debtor by force, if he encountered him in the street, and give it to the creditor. These restrictions only apply where the debt has been incurred through loans, but if the amount was owed for wages or for the hire of livestock or goods, or was rent for living quarters, or for the guarantee of a debt — in all these cases it is permissible to seize a pledge by force, even without a court order, or to enter the debtor's house and take a pledge, since the Scriptural passage refers only to outstanding loans. Where the money owed for wages etc. was converted into a loan, these seizures are prohibited, since the debt now assumes the nature of a loan. The conversion occurs at the time when a due date for payment is set (see *Choshen Mishpat*, Chap. 67). Others hold the opinion that when the creditor enters the total sum in his ledger, the amount becomes converted into a loan. These qualifications refer to the prohibition against entering the debtor's house. However, seizing a widow's possessions or seizing utensils used in the preparation of food is, according to some authorities, prohibited under all circumstances (Ibid. Par. 14).

(3)   The creditor is also forbidden to send his agent to the borrower's home to seize a pledge. Whether he is permitted to send his agent to the debtor's home to request a pledge has not been clarified (see *Nethiv Hachesed*). The creditor may send his agent to request the debtor to bring him a pledge for the amount of the loan. In this instance, the agent is allowed to enter the debtor's home, since he only comes to deliver a message. It appears that if the debtor were then to hand a pledge to the agent, the agent would be allowed to accept it, since by so doing he becomes the agent of the debtor and not of the creditor.

(4)   All that we have written in Paragraphs 1 and 2 refer to ordinary articles taken as pledges, but not to utensils used in the

preparation of food. These latter may not be taken by the court messenger, and certainly not by the lender, even if he were to stand outside the debtor's house, since Scripture declares (Deut. 24.6): "No man shall take the mill or the upper millstone to pledge, for he takes the man's life to pledge." The prohibition is not restricted to these articles only, but to all utensils used in the preparation of food, such as: kneading troughs, pots for cooking, the *shochet's* knife and the like, since all are included in the category of "For he takes the man's life to pledge." Certainly if the messenger of the court or the lender were to enter the borrower's house and take such articles as pledges, he would all the more be guilty — since he would be transgressing this special prohibition in addition to the commandment forbidding entry into the debtor's house to seize a pledge.

(5)   If a debtor owns five of one kind of food utensil, the creditor is not allowed to take any one of them as a pledge. If he does, he would be guilty for each one separately. If the debtor uses only one of these, then it is permissible to take the others in pledge, provided, of course, that the court messenger makes the seizure outside the debtor's house, as has been explained previously (Pars. 1 and 2).

(6)   No pledge may be seized from a widow, whether she be rich or poor, whether the article is used in the preparation of food or not, since it is written (Deut. 24.17): "Nor take the widow's raiment to pledge." Scripture did not intend to restrict the prohibition to clothes alone, but to all the widow's possessions. Even the messenger of the court, outside her house, is forbidden to take anything from her. If he enters her house and seizes a pledge, he has transgressed two negative commandments of the Torah: "You shall not go into his house to take the pledge" and also "Nor take the widow's raiment to pledge."

(7)   All the prohibitions mentioned above apply only when the pledge is taken not at the time the loan was made. At the time of the

giving of the loan, however, it is permissible to enter the lender's home, to take utensils used for food, and to accept pledges from a widow, since the borrower is agreeable to taking the loan on these terms. If the borrower, on his own initiative and outside his house, offers a pledge, it may be accepted at any time, even if it consists of food utensils or a widow's possessions. See our remarks in *Nethiv Hachesed*, subsection 4, that the same rule applies where the borrower calls out to the lender and invites him to enter his house to take delivery of the pledge. This, too, is altogether permissible. The creditor may not, however, select the pledge; he must accept whatever the lender proffers him. The creditor is forbidden to make any use of the pledge, even where the debtor gave it of his own free will.

(8)   Know that it makes no difference, in this connection, whether the money is lent by individuals, or from public charity funds by their treasurers, or else from a *gemiluth chesed* sum which one person had lent to another without a pledge. If the debtor failed, in these instances, to pay on the due date, the treasurer or his representative is forbidden to enter the debtor's house to take a pledge, and all aforementioned laws apply to this case.

(9)   One authority holds that the messenger of the court is only forbidden to enter the debtor's house to take a pledge to hold as security for the repayment of the debt, either before or after the date for repayment falls due. He does not wish, for some reason or other, to take the article as repayment for the debt, but merely to hold it as security. If, however, the debt falls due, the creditor demands repayment, and the debtor resists (he has the means but conceals his assets), then the messenger of the court has the right to enter his house and levy distraint. To repay a debt is a mitzvah, no less than *sukkah, lulav* and *tefillin*, the observance of which the *Beth Din* may enforce by administering lashes to the recalcitrant to within an inch

of his life. (So here, too, the messenger may enter the debtor's house and seize the pledge in repayment — Tr.) Where the defaulting debtor has no assets, he is not compelled to hire himself out or to work in order to pay his debt. "The children of Israel are My slaves and not the slaves of others" — *Hashem* holds a prior bill of servitude. The *Sha'ar Hamishpat* (q.v.) states that certain authorities hold that only the court is forbidden to apply force, but he himself is morally bound to seek employment in order to pay off his debt.

8

THE POSITIVE COMMANDMENT
TO RETURN THE PLEDGE

(1) Now we shall elucidate the details of the positive commandment ordering the restoring of the pledge. It is written (Deut. 24.12): "And if he be a poor man, you shall not sleep with his pledge; you shall surely restore the pledge to him when the sun goes down, that he may sleep in his garment." Now *Chazal* have explained the intent of the Biblical command (Bava Metzia 114b): "You shall not sleep while the pledge is still in your hand; return it when the sun goes down so that he may have it to sleep on." The reference is to night clothes which the creditor must return to the debtor for each evening. In the morning the creditor resumes possession of them once more. Another verse states (Exod. 22.25): "You shall return it to him until the sun goes down." This law refers to a day garment which the creditor must return to the debtor for the entire day, until the sun goes down, at which time the creditor will regain it. The creditor must fulfill these conditions every day and night. It may then be asked: what benefit does the possession of the pledge bestow? The debtor is put to shame, since the pledge is returned each day. He will then hurry to obtain the money and pay his debt. A pledge also saves the debt from being cancelled by the Sabbatical year, since debts protected by pledges are not subject to the *shemittah* remission. In the event of the debtor's death, this pledge would not be regarded as the movable property of a deceased, which is not subject to any creditor's lien. Payment is exacted from the pledge.

When the creditor returns the pledge, the debtor is obliged to bless him, as it says (Deut. ibid.): "That he may sleep in his garment and bless you" (*Sifrei*). If the creditor does not restore the pledge at the proper times, he transgresses both a negative and a positive commandment, in addition to violating the prohibition against entering the debtor's house to take a pledge if he had taken the pledge without the authorization of the *Beth Din*. The above-mentioned requirements do not only refer to a poor debtor. If a basic necessity, such as bedclothes, was taken in pledge from a rich person and he has no others, then the creditor would transgress the positive and negative commandments if he did not comply with the conditions mentioned here. The Torah merely refers to the most frequently occurring instances, since the poor person normally has only one night garment. Even though the debtor had not requested its return, the article must be restored at the proper time. (This law differs from the case of a hired worker [explained further on in Chap. 9] where no transgression is committed unless the wages are claimed, since Scripture there makes this stipulation, as is found in the *Gemara*.)

(2) If the creditor wishes to substitute another garment, not the one taken in pledge, for the debtor to sleep in, he has, it appears, not thereby fulfilled the positive Scriptural command of restoring the pledge, since Scripture specifies (ibid.): "And he may sleep in *his* garment and bless you." The same law applies to the day garment. (The Vilna Gaon remarks in his notes on *Choshen Mishpat* [Chap. 72, Par. 11] that if the creditor had substituted some other article for the debtor's pledge, he has not effectively complied with the law. See ibid.) The inference may be drawn that tools, too, which have to be returned for use by day, may not be exchanged.

(3) If the creditor had failed to restore the article immediately at sundown, his obligation, nevertheless, remains in force until the morning. In our context this would mean until the time people

customarily rise, since then the time for him to "sleep in his garment" has ended (see *Nethiv Hachesed*). The same principle applies to a day garment. If the creditor fails to restore it in the morning, at the time people normally rise, his obligation nevertheless remains in force until the end of the day, as Scripture ordains: "Until the sun goes down, you shall return it to him." Sundown here refers to the time the stars appear, the beginning of the usual time for retiring at night. Then the individual no longer needs his day clothes.

(4)   The law of returning a pledge applies, irrespective of whether the lender exacted the pledge from the borrower through a messenger of the court or whether he seized the pledge illegally on his own, or whether the borrower himself took the pledge to the lender. In all these cases it is a mitzvah to restore the pledge at the time of its use to the borrower, since he is poor and needs it. Hence, the day clothes must be restored for the day, and the night clothes or bedding for the night. The craftsman's tools of trade must be restored for the day, so that he can ply his trade; the creditor resumes possession at night when the stars appear. If the creditor transgressed and took food utensils or the clothes of a widow to pledge, or if these were given voluntarily, the obligation to return them, when they are required for use, still obtains. Other authorities rule that these items must be restored to their owners immediately, if the creditor has transgressed and taken them. All these remarks apply where the pledge was taken at a time other than when the loan was made. If the lender took them at the time of making the loan, he is not obliged to return them, since they were freely given. The same ruling would apply even when the borrower gave the pledge not at the time the loan was made, as long as he gave it to the lender of his own initiative, and expressly consented to forego having it returned to him when these were required for use. The creditor is then not obliged to return the pledge. How pledges should be dealt with when repayment falls due and the debtor is delinquent, and also the laws of

levying distraint on the debtor's property, are explained in *Choshen Mishpat* (Chap. 73, Par. 12 ff.; Chap. 97, Par. 23).

(5)   Some authorities rule that the law pertaining to the restoration of pledges also applies when the article was taken as security from a guarantor or as security for the payment of wages, or for the hire of an animal, or rent for a dwelling, although the prohibition against entering the debtor's house does not affect a guarantor and the like, as has been explained in Chapter 7. Nevertheless the positive commandment of restoring the pledge applies here as well. Others hold that the law pertaining to the return of pledges does not apply in these instances.

(6)   If a person had promised to give the sum of money to the poor, and the charity treasurer exacted a pledge from him to ensure the fulfillment of his promise, the treasurer does not have to return the pledge at the required times, even though he had transgressed and taken a food utensil or a widow's garment. The poor receive their share from Heaven and are classed as *Hekdesh*. They are not included in the law governing the return of pledges, as is evident in the *Gemara*. According to the first opinion cited above (Par. 5), even here the treasurer must return a pledge consisting of a widow's garment or food utensil immediately.

(7)   The above law applies as long as the treasurer had not received the money and taken custody of it as the agent of the poor. However, if he had transgressed and lent out charity of *gemiluth chesed* funds to someone and then when the debt fell due and the debtor was delinquent exacted a pledge from him, all the laws of returning the pledge apply.

INTRODUCTION TO LAWS OF WAGES

I have further seen fit to append to these laws the regulations governing paying the hire of laborers, since this matter is of supreme importance. It involves a number of explicit Torah prohibitions. Yet many individuals treat these laws lightly, because of our many sins. They find it easy to defer payment for some minor excuse, such as being too lazy to go and withdraw their deposits, or to change a large bill so as to pay the worker on time. Legally, one is obliged to comply with all the regulations, even where the worker is well-to-do. How much more careful must the employer be where the worker is poor, to pay him on time, so that he and his household will have the wherewithal to live, as Scripture states (Deut. 24.15): —"In the same day you shall give him his hire, and neither shall the sun go down upon it, for he is poor and sets his soul upon it; lest he cry out against you unto God, and it shall be sin in you."

Come now and see what the *Zohar* (Lev. 19.13) has to say: "Why does Scripture state: 'The wages of a hired servant shall not abide with you all night until the morning'? The reason for this last injunction is to be found in the verse (Deut. 24.15): 'In his day you shall give him his hire, and the sun shall not go down upon it,' that is to say, that you be not gathered from the world on his account before your time comes. From this we learn another thing, that if one restores the soul of a poor man, even if his own time has arrived to depart from the world, God restores his soul and gives him a further lease on life. To withhold the wages of a poor man is like taking his life and the life of his household. As he (the employer) diminishes their souls, so God diminishes his days, and cuts off his soul from the other world. For all the breaths which issue from his (the poor man's) mouth for the whole of that day ascend and stand before the Almighty, and afterwards his soul and the souls of his household ascend and stand in those breaths. Thus even if length of days and many blessings had been decreed for that man, they are all withdrawn, nor does his soul mount aloft. Therefore R. Abba said: God save us from them and their plaint! And the same is true even if it is a rich man, and his right is withheld from him, and surely if he is a poor man. Hence R. Hamnuna, when a hired worker had finished his task, used to give him his wage and say to him: Take your soul which you have entrusted to my hand! Take your deposit! And even if the other asked him to keep it for him, he was unwilling to do so, saying: It is not fitting that your body shall be deposited with me, still less your soul, which should be deposited only with God, as it is written (Ps. 31.6): 'Into Your hand I commit my spirit.' " (See further, *Zohar*, Ibid.)

Now the verse we have quoted previously admonishes even in the case where the employer gives the worker his due hire, but merely defers payment and does not remit on time. How much greater is the warning where the employer withholds the hire altogether, and does not pay at all — or else, deducts even a single cent from the amount agreed upon in the first place. The employer here is guilty of actual robbery. He transgresses the prohibition (Lev. 19.13): "You shall not oppress your neighbor, nor rob him." So the *Gemara* explains (Bava Metzia 61 a/b; 111a). Through the medium of His prophets, too, the Almighty has issued a stern warning on this subject, and has said (Mal. 3.5): "And I will come near to you to judgment; and I will be a swift witness against the sorcerers and against the adulterers, and against false swearers; and against those that oppress the hireling in his wages." As for the statement "And I shall come near ... a swift witness," this indicates that the Almighty Himself acts both as judge and witness, so as to speedily avenge the opperession of withholding the wages of a hired hand. As the *Gemara* (Sukkah 29b) puts it: "On account of four things do householders lose their property: On account of those who defer payment of a laborer's hire; and on account of those who withhold the hired laborer's wage. ." (Deferring = telling him to go and come again; withholding = not paying at all — Rashi.)

Now because of our many sins, people find it easy to reduce the hired man's wages. They are unaware that this pertains to their very souls for they transgress Torah prohibitions. Frequently, too, because of our many sins, hired laborers knock at the doors of their employers day and night, yet no one pays attention to them, especially where the transaction involves a small amount. They fail to take heed that in Torah jurisprudence, it makes no difference whether a case involves one cent or $100. Yet many (of the guilty) are honest and virtuous individuals who fulfill all other Torah commandments punctiliously. In observing the commandments concerning the payment of paying the hired laborer on time, however, they are neglectful, because of our many sins, even where all that is needed is some effort. Now I have realized that all this occurs because of extreme ignorance of the law. If the individuals concerned were aware of its importance, they would take the most meticulous care to pay on time, thereby to fulfill the positive commandment of "In the same day shall you pay his hire" (and also to avoid transgressing the prohibitions in this matter) with the same diligence as every one in Israel performs the other mitzvoth of the Torah which have a set time, such as *Sukkah, Lulav,* etc. Have you ever seen a Jew deferring the recitation of the *berachah* on the *Shofar* or *Lulav* till evening? On the contrary, every Jew seeks to be early, and performs the commandment in the morning. He is happy to have succeeded in fulfilling the commandment of His Creator, blessed be He. Yet how overpowering is the evil inclination in respect of this mitzvah, which is no less a positive commandment, and to which the Torah has added several prohibitions as well! I have therefore taken the subject to heart and, with the help of God Who grants man knowledge, have searched for and collected all the details of this law so as to alert everyone to comply properly with all its requirements. This I have begun with the help of my Rock and my Redeemer.

9

LAWS OF PAYING HIRED WORKERS ON TIME

(1) It is written in the Torah (Lev. 19.13): "The wages of a hired worker shall not abide with you all night (*lo talin*) until the morning." Another verse ordains (Deut. 24.15): "In the same day you shall give him his hire; the sun shall not go down upon it." *Chazal* have explained (Bava Metzia 110b) that the first verse refers to one who works by the day. He must be paid during the ensuing night. If the employer withholds payment until daybreak, he then commits *bal talin,* the transgression of withholding wages. The second verse refers to one who works by the night. The time for paying his wages is the whole of the ensuing day. If he had not been paid by sundown, then the employer transgresses this negative commandment and also the positive commandment of "In the same day you shall give him his hire." One should take care to pay such wages before sunset, when it is surely day — since afterwards twilight sets in. If the employer had not paid the worker by sunset, he should at least do so before the stars appear, since immediately afterwards he will certainly be guilty of violating both a negative and a positive commandment.

(2) The rule that the night worker may be paid during the ensuing day applies only if he was hired to work all night until daybreak. However, if he was hired only for a few hours, and completed his task before daybreak, then the payment of his wages may not be delayed beyond daybreak. The same principle applies to one who

works by the day. If he was not hired for a full day's work but only for a few hours, and his task was completed before sunset, the payment of his wages may not be delayed beyond sunset (as was explained at the end of Par. 1). In our times, workmen normally cease working by sunset, hence the employer should make haste to pay them before the stars appear, since this employment would be considered hourly work (see *Nethiv Hachesed*). If the workman remained at his job, even though not obliged by present usage, until the stars appeared, then the employer would have all night to pay his wages. If the workman requested his pay on a Friday, when it is the normal practice to stop work a short time before sunset, the employer should hasten to pay him if he has the means, and thereby fulfill the positive commandment of "In the same day you shall give him his hire."

(3)   Know that not only where the workman was engaged for a few hours, but even if he was hired to perform the most trivial task for which the hire is a mere *perutah,* he is still classed as a hired worker and all the relevant laws apply to him. Some authorities rule that even if the task was worth less than a *perutah,* to delay paying his wages constitutes a violation. People are, because of our many sins, delinquent in this matter.

(4)   If workers were hired by the week, or the month, or the year, or for a seven-year period, and they completed their assigned task by day, they must be paid before sundown on the same day. The same principle applies where the assignment was completed at night. The workers must then be paid before dawn on that same night.

(5)   The same laws apply irrespective of whether a person, an animal or a chattel was hired, since Scripture states: "The wages of a hired worker shall not abide with you" and any type of hired work that is "with you" is included. As for land rentals, legal opinions dif-

fer. The Vilna Gaon (see his notes) tends to rule strictly, following the discussion in the *Gemara*. Indeed, the *Sifra* states explicitly that the term widening the Scriptural reference *(ribui)* extends the application to land rentals as well. I subsequently found that the *Sha'ar Hamishpat* has given the same ruling. Hence one should surely exercise great care in paying rent for houses (see *Nethiv Hachesed*). Similar care must be observed when a minor is hired, to whom all the above laws apply.

(6)   Where the workman died, the son does not inherit his father's rights in respect of the employer committing a violation if he withholds the wages beyond the times specified above.

(7)   The employer does not transgress the prohibition unless he has the money to pay the worker, since Scripture ordains: "The wages of a hired worker shall not abide with you," "with you" implying that you have it with you. If the employer has given a pledge or a loan to a third party and this has fallen due, he is considered as having the money with him, since he can recover this sum. The *Shittah Mekubetzeth* quoting the *Ritva* records that if the employer has food which is meant to be sold, he is regarded as having the money with him, since he can sell his merchandise. The same conclusion may be inferred from the *Sefer Hachinuch* (588). The employer should certainly, if he can, borrow money to pay his worker and thereby carry out the positive commandment, especially if the worker is poor, where by giving him his wages on time the employer upholds him and saves him from becoming dependent upon charity. (See *Nethiv Hachesed,* Chap. 1, subsection 20).

(8)   If an employer hired two workers and has sufficient money only to pay one, it appears that he should divide the amount between the two. He does not commit any transgression, since this is all the money he has. Even if one of them demanded his wages before the

other, the employer should still retain half for the second, since the latter will certainly demand his wages. The *Gemara* declares (Shevuoth 45a): "It is a presumption in law that a hired workman does not leave his wages unclaimed." If he knows that the other will not mind, he may pay the first his complete wages at this time. The principle applies where the two workmen are either both rich or both poor. What the law requires, when one is rich and the other poor, will be explained in Chap. 10.

(9) Once the worker has completed his work, the employer must avoid investing the money needed to pay the wages, even though the worker has not yet claimed his hire. It is certainly forbidden to invest it after the workman has made his claim. The employer then violates the commandment of "In the same day you shall give him his hire." Every reasonable person should take steps, even before the worker has completed his assigned task, to guard against such an eventuality.

(10) If the employer has the wherewithal, the worker must be paid his full wages at the proper time. Should he fail to pay in full, he transgresses the prohibition: "The wages ... shall not abide ..." Similarly, if the employer does not have the full amount at hand, he is obliged to give the workman as much as he does have. Otherwise he violates the commandment.

(11) Know that every violation of the employer mentioned in this chapter is committed only where the worker claimed his wages and the employer failed to pay. If the workman did not demand his wages, then the employer has committed no transgression by not paying, even if he does have the money available. Here the worker tacitly allows him to retain the money. Other authorities rule that even if the worker made no claim, the employer is still obliged to pay his hire in time. In this case, however, the Scriptural commandment

is not violated by non-compliance (*Sha'ar Hamishpat;* the same has been shown by the *Chevel Yosef*). If the employer had not the means to pay when the worker demanded his hire, but subsequently acquired the money before the due date had expired, he is obliged to take it to the worker forthwith or at least to notify the worker to come and fetch his wages, to avoid violating the negative commandment. Where someone had hired an animal or chattels for his needs, and the task for which the hire was made had been completed, he must hasten to pay for the hire within the limits set by the law. Here, the fact that no claim was made is no tacit permission to retain the hire, since the owner did not know that the work had been completed, and he therefore could not make his claim.

(12) Once the due date for repayment has passed, the employer does not add to his transgression of the Scriptural prohibition against withholding payment (*bal talin*). Nevertheless, he is obliged to pay immediately. As long as he delays, he transgresses the Rabbinical injunction (Prov. 3.28): "Say not to your neighbor: Go and come again and tomorrow I will give; and you have it with you."

(13) Where the worker is aware that the employer normally has not the money available before the next market day, the employer does not transgress the prohibition, even where he does have the money available and the workman claimed his hire on the first day of his employment. Here the worker had, from the beginning, abandoned hope of collecting his wages before the next market day. If the market day subsequently passed, the employer violates this prohibition (Prov. 3.28): "Say not to your neighbor: Go and come again and tomorrow I will give." The same principle applies to those who are accustomed to pay only after the correct amount of wages due has been calculated. They do not transgress until the payroll has been computed, since here the workers had agreed to this procedure from the start.

10

LAWS PERTAINING TO PAYING WAGES ON TIME

(1)   If a person contracted with a craftsman and gave him his coat to repair, then as long as the garment is still in the possession of the craftsman, the owner does not violate any prohibition. Where the craftsman returned it to him at midday, then the owner will violate the commandment of "In the same day you shall pay his hire," if payment is delayed beyond sundown. Similarly, if the craftsman returned the garment at night, the owner will transgress at daybreak. Work contracts are governed by the same law as day laborers, as far as paying in time is concerned.

(2)   Where someone had instructed his agent to go and hire workers, and the agent, when hiring them, stipulated that his principal was responsible for their hire, then the prohibition against withholding wages does not apply to either the principal or the agent — the owner, because he did not hire them and hence the workmen are not his hirelings; the agent, because he had notified them that his principal, and not he, would be responsible for their hire. Even if he had not expressly made this stipulation, he would still be under no obligation, since the workers were aware that they would not be employed by him, as will be explained. Nevertheless, the principal transgresses the Rabbinic injunction: "Say not to your neighbor: Go and come again . . ." when he tries to avoid paying them on time. If he is preoccupied and has no time, he does not violate this injunction.

(3)   Even though the agent had specified that he was merely acting on behalf of the principal, and that they would not be working for
him, if he had assumed the responsibility of paying their hire, he
would transgress the obligation if the workers were not paid in time.
If the agent had hired them without making any stipulations, neither
stating that he or that his principal was responsible, the law will depend upon whether the workers knew or did not know that they were
not working for him. In the first event, he would not be, in the second, he would be responsible for their hire, and commit the violation if they were not paid on time.

(4)   The law stated so far applies to the case of an ordinary agent.
However, where someone acted as the administrator of another's
property, then even though the workers knew that they were not
working for the agent's benefit, he is still considered as one who assumes responsibility for their hire, even though he made no explicit
stipulation when he hired them. He is therefore liable if he withholds
their wages beyond the time limit. If a woman who has a husband
conducts business on her own, and hires workmen without expressly
accepting responsibility for their hire, she is nevertheless liable if she
withholds their pay.

(5)   Where the employer gave his workers a draft on a bank or
other agency (where, for instance, the worker needed money and the
employer instructed his agent or banker to advance the money on his
behalf), and the banker agreed to honor the draft and the worker
agreed to this procedure, then the employer will not be liable if their
wages are withheld, even though he had not previously deposited
money with the bank, and the banker now refuses to honor the draft.
The employer is bound by the law where the wages are "with you",
not where they are held by the banker.

(6)   The above exclusion applies only to the prohibition: "The
wages of a hired worker shall not abide with you." However, if the

worker later changed his mind and wished to be paid directly by the employer and not by the banker, the worker is entitled to retract what he agreed to at first, and may claim directly from the employer. He may obviously change his mind where the banker refuses to honor the draft, since he had not agreed to accept the arrangement in such event; and he may do so even where the banker does not refuse to cash the draft.

(7)   The above limitation applies where the worker had not expressly discharged the employer from his obligation to pay, even if the banker would fail to honor the draft, or where the workman had not bound himself to this condition by a *kinyan* (symbolic act of acceptance — Tr.). Where he had, the worker would have no further claim on his employer.

(8)   If the employer had hired two workmen, one poor, the other not, and the employer only had sufficient money available to pay one of them his hire, then the poor takes precedence, since Scripture has stated (ibid.): "For he is poor," and *Chazal* have declared the intent of the verse to be that the poor takes precedence over the rich. If one is poor and the other indigent (*evyon*, derived from *avo*, signifying want, and the inability to satisfy that want) the poor comes first (since the indigent is accustomed to the shame of poverty). If one is rich and the other indigent, then the indigent takes preference.

(9)   Where the two are both either poor or indigent and one is related to the employer, he is not thereby entitled to any preference.

(10)   Know that where the poor takes preference, he does so even if the rich were to claim his hire first, since the poor will almost certainly come later to claim his hire when it is due, as we have stated: It is a presumption of the law, that the workman does not leave his hire unclaimed.

(11)   If the two workers either were both poor or had means, and one had worked as his day laborer the day before, so that the time for violating the transgression of not paying his hire had passed, while the second had worked for him this day, then the employer would be obliged to pay the second workman first, before the time limit passes. He should pay the first worker later, as soon as he procures the money. Here, possibly, even a rich worker would take precedence over a poor one.

(12)   The workman normally expects to be paid on time, as Scripture points out (Deut. 24.15): "He sets his heart on it." Hence an employer should never hire a workman where he knows for sure that he will be unable to pay the hire on time, unless he notified the worker beforehand and the workman accepted his terms, or else the local usage is to pay workmen on market days when money is abundant — as explained at the end of Chapter 9. For this reason, an employer intending to leave on a journey, who will not return to pay wages on time, should arrange, before he leaves, that the hire be available for his employee when payment falls due.

[(13)   does not appear in the original. Either the paragraph was inadvertently omitted in the printed edition or a mistake was made in numbering — Tr.].

(14)   What has been written in the last two chapters has only dealt with wages deferred and not paid on time. If the employer, however, retains the wages and has no intention of paying (or even if he so withholds even one *perutah* of what he owes], he transgresses the prohibition (Lev. 19.13): "You shall not oppress your neighbor nor rob him." This act constitutes robbery as well, as the Gemara lays down, and the guilty party is thereby disqualified from giving testimony in any trial. *Chazal* have declared (Bava Metzia 112a): "Whoever withholds the wages of an employee is like one who

deprives him of his life and transgresses six commandments — five negative and one positive: [(a) "You shall not oppress your neighbour" (Lev. 19.13), (b) "Neither shall you rob him" (Ibid.), (c) "The wages of a hired workman shall not abide with you" (Ibid.), (d) "You shall not oppress a hired person that is poor" (Deut. 24.13), (e) "Neither shall the sun go down on it" (Deut. 24.15), and the positive commandment of "In the same day you shall give him his hire" (Ibid.)]. The *Gemara* (Bava Metzia 111a) and the *Zohar* (Kedoshim) have gone to great length in dealing with this matter. Hence, whoever is concerned for his soul should heed himself exceedingly in this matter and so will receive his due reward and recompense.

I shall, in passing, quote some advice appearing in my booklet, *Sefath Tamim,* covering the prohibition against robbery and withholding the wages of a hired laborer: Everyone engaging another to perform a task for him for pay should first have the worker agree on the price. Otherwise one may very easily become guilty of robbery or withholding the wages of a hired worker, unless he is ready to squander his money to extricate himself from any doubt. Does not every person require hundreds of tasks to be performed for him each year? Very frequently it happens that after the completion of the task, an argument ensues between the employee and the employer regarding the payment of the fee. When they part, each feels in his heart that he has been robbed by the other. It is only that he is reluctant to argue, but he has by no means wholeheartedly relinquished his claim. At other times, the two quarrel with each other. Legally, all such contracts are determined by local usage, depending on time and place. Now if an employer pays a single penny less than the local custom requires, the Torah brands him as a *gazlan,* a robber, and as one who withholds the wages of a hired hand. Yet who can really determine what local custom requires in each particular instance? Hence anyone wishing to fulfill his obligation, without any misgivings, would always be forced to pay his worker whatever the latter demands. This would cause great difficulty. Hence the person wishing to do what is right in the eyes of Heaven will fix the price with his workman in advance, and so remove all doubt. The workman, for his part, will charge less, since the employer will still have the choice of offering the assignment to someone else. A *Talmid Chacham* will certainly follow this procedure, since otherwise, if he refuses to pay what the worker demands, he may very easily be guilty, in addition to the suspicion of robbery and withholding the wages of a hired hand, of profaning the Divine Name, for the workman will proclaim that he had been cheated by a *Talmid Chacham.*

II

1

CHESED EXPLAINED

How greatly should one cling to the virtue of *chesed*! The extent of the required attachment is defined in the verse (Micah 6.8): "It has been told to you, O man, what is good and what God requires of you: Only to act justly and to love *chesed* (kindness) . . ." At first sight, it would seem that it should have been sufficient for Scripture either to read: "to act with justice and kindness" or else "to love justice and kindness." Moreover, by using the expression, "It has been told to you . . ." Scripture must have intended to convey an idea which man would be unable to discover on his own.

Now everyone knows that it is very important to act justly. This truth is clearly revealed in the **Sidrah, Mishpatim,** in the Torah. *Chesed,* as well, is obviously important, as many verses bear out, as has been shown in our introduction. However, the true meaning of the Scriptural intent becomes evident from the statement of *Chazal* (Sanhedrin 7a): "If a person's coat has been taken from him as a result of a court verdict, he should sing for joy." We can illustrate this statement by a story.

A band of rebels lived in a certain city. Many joined them. To strengthen their ties with one another, they agreed to wear similar garments, all dyed the same color. They would thus be set off from the rest of the population and become recognizable to one another even from far off. One day they crowded into the local tavern and drank heavily. Some of them refused to pay for their drinks, and the owner would not allow them to go until they had left their clothes

77

behind as security for their debts. They stalked out angrily. Shortly afterwards the conspiracy along with their mode of identification was disclosed to the king. Their activities were investigated and all those who wore the uniform were captured. Their possessions were forfeited and they perished. The only exceptions were those who were unable to wear their uniforms. They were not caught, and so were saved. They said to each other: "We thought that the tavern owner had done us harm by forcing us to leave our clothes behind. In truth he did us a great favor. He saved our lives. Let us go and applaud him for what happened now. For the future, let us make up our minds not to follow the evil ways of our friends, so that we avoid being caught like them."

So, in our lives, every person must realize that the appropriation of another's property may cause him to lose even that part of his possessions which he did honestly acquire, especially when even his very clothes are not untainted by dishonest or forceful acquisition, as we have learned from the words of *Chazal*. Well have they stated, then: "When the court concludes that the clothes a person is wearing were dishonestly acquired and therefore orders that they be restored to their rightful owner, the loser should sing for joy, since otherwise Heaven might have confiscated his property and he might have become bereft of all his possessions."

Now we may proceed to understand the verse, "It has been told to you . . ." quoted above. When a person devotes all his energy to the acquisition of property, and takes no care that his gains be free of the taint of robbery, forceful expropriation, dishonest dealing and the like, he may delude himself into believing that, at least for the present, he is doing himself good by his exertions, and that the reckoning will only come at the end, in the world above. The prophet, therefore, enlightened us by saying: "It has been told to you, O man, what is good." He intended to convey that, contrary to the common belief that it is good for man to amass wealth, what is really to his monetary advantage is to act justly — to scrutinize all his transactions so as to ensure that his profits were acquired through means approved by Torah law. In this way, he will make certain that his possessions remain with him. This is what Scripture means by "only to do justice."

Next the prophet adds, "to love *chesed.*" He intends to convey that no one should deem it sufficient to ensure that his possessions are free from the taint of dishonesty, and believe that they will, therefore, remain with him, and that good will be bestowed on him on this account. He is also to dispense kindness and charity proportionate to his means. Otherwise, God forbid, his wealth might gradually be reduced, as is related in *Kethuvoth* 66b concerning Nakdimon ben Gurion. (See ibid.)

As for the choice of words, "to act justly and *love chesed,*" rather than "to act with justice and *chesed,*" the prophet has thereby drawn our attention to a new and important lesson, to an area where almost everyone is at fault. Indeed, we all perform acts of kindness. But we are kind only under pressure. When a person in distress, needing our favor, turns to us once, and again a second time, we find it difficult to avoid him, so we extend help to him. Even then we act not at all willingly or kind-heartedly. So the prophet exhorts us: "What does God require of you: only to *love* kindness. You should not think that by your occasional acts of kindness you have discharged your duty completely." Instead, one must possess a *love* for this mitzvah.

Obviously a great difference lies between what a person does because of pressure and what he does out of love. We see how we, ourselves, act towards our children, in pursuit of food and clothing, in marriage, and in all that is motivated by love. Here every person ranges far beyond his duty. A father seeks to bring benefit to his son, even when the latter has not asked for it. He is happy and in good spirits when he does so. So in this case, if a person really loves this trait of *chesed,* he will search for the ways and means to do good to his fellow man, and he will act generously. And as for the many aspects of this virtue (which we shall, please God, explain further on), he will seek to fulfill them all out of love and not through compulsion.

See how great this virtue is. In our blessing of thanksgiving to God at the end of our *Tefillah,* our prayers read: "For with the light of Your countenance, You have given us, O *Hashem,* our God, a living Torah and the love of *chesed.*" The light of His countenance, blessed be He, was revealed to us at Mount Sinai. As Scripture has it: "You were taught to know that *Hashem* is God." Now *Chazal* have asserted that God, blessed be He, then opened up all the heavens and nether regions and revealed that He was the One ruling them all. At that same time several fundamental truths were also disclosed: that the Torah is the source of existence of heaven and earth; for its sake all endures, and without it all existence would cease, as *Chazal* have declared (Avodah Zarah 3a): "God stipulated with the creation, 'If Israel will accept the Torah, well and good. If not, I shall make you revert to nothingness.' " Now if the world would be devoid of Torah for a single instant, the entire creation would be reduced to non-existence, since the Torah is the source, in the upper regions, of all existence, as the holy books quote from the *Zohar.*

At that holy convocation, too, the manner in which man is expected to pursue the virtue of *chesed* and to love it with all his life also became clear to all who were present. Then they perceived with their prophetic insight how the continuance of the creation is maintained; they grasped how existence, in its entirety, its permanence, its sustenance, is totally contingent upon the *chesed* of God, blessed be He, which pervades the entire universe, as Scripture declares (Ps. 136.25): "He provides for all flesh; His *chesed* endures forever," and in another verse: "The *chesed* of God fills the land." Now, were the Holy One, blessed be He, to deal with His creatures only in accordance with pure justice, God forbid, the world could not exist even for an instant, as *Chazal* have stated in *Midrash Tehillim* in reference to the verses (Ps. 89.1,2): "Maskil of Ethan the Ezrachi, I will sing of the *chasadim* of *Hashem,* God, forever . . ." They asked Ethan: What holds up the earth? He replied, *Chesed,* as it is said

(Isa. 16.5): 'The throne shall be held up by *chesed.'* To what may this be compared? — to a stool. One of its four legs became loose. A pebble was placed under the leg and it held firm. So, as it were, is the throne of God. It became infirm. How did God prop it up?—with *chesed.* He declared then: I said the world would be built on *chesed."* Hence man should always cling to this trait. Through its merit, he will survive both in this world and the next, as will be explained further on by reference to Scriptural passages and Rabbinic dicta.

2

THE REASON FOR THE TORAH URGING MAN TO LOVE THIS VIRTUE

In this chapter we shall elucidate the reason why God, blessed be He, so strongly urged man to acquire this virtue, that every section of the Torah is pervaded by it, as was explained in the introduction. The reason why man is obliged to possess a love of this virtue was explained in Chapter 1. Here we shall proceed to elucidate the subject in various ways, with the help of God.

Scripture (Gen 1.27) records that, "God created man in His image." The commentators take the statement to refer to God's attributes. He gave His creatures the power to emulate His *middoth;* to do good and to act with kindness towards their fellow men, as Scripture has it (Ps. 145.9): "God is good to all . . ." (Ibid. 136.25) "He gives food to all flesh, for His *chesed* endures forever." The existence of the entire world then depends on this virtue, as is shown further on. Hence, whoever follows in this path will bear the stamp of God on his person; while whoever refrains from exercising this virtue and questions himself, "Why should I do good to others?" removes himself completely from God, blessed be He.

Now when we examine closely, it becomes evident that the existence of all mankind is dependent upon the virtues of charity and kindness, for each and every man is confronted by changing circumstances during his lifetime. On each occasion he needs cooperation and assistance to cope with his particular situation. How does this happen? Sometimes one requires financial assistance from someone else, perhaps the loan of a sum of money. Even a rich man may find himself in this position. Or else, one may need the help of some person in finding employment or a profitable commercial enterprise. Almost all of mankind are thus affected. (This is the mitzvah of "You shall uphold him," "And your brother shall live with you.") Sometimes one needs to be helped by another's presence as, when he celebrates a happy occasion, he requires others to share his joy with him (for instance in bringing joy to bride and groom), for man can never be happy alone. When someone is sad, he is in need of the strength and comfort extended by others (here we have the mitzvah of comforting the mourners and the like, where the burden of a person's sorrow is lightened); or else he needs the relief they provide from his cares, which might otherwise cause him to become ill. Sometimes when one is on a journey far from his home, he requires help with the transport of his merchandise (the mitzvah of loading and unloading). If the traveller has to stop in the homes of others, they should proffer him the proper hospitality befitting his dignity (the mitzvah of hospitality to wayfarers, which extends even to those who are not poor, as is elucidated in Part III, Chapter I). When a person is ill, he needs the companionship of visitors, who take an interest in his condition, and who may even help to hasten his cure (the mitzvah of visiting the sick). And after the person has completed the course of his life and has died, he certainly becomes dependent on others for that act of charity which can never be repaid. The rule is: the world cannot exist without this virtue of *chesed*. Therefore the Torah has specified, time and again, that everyone must exert himself to embody this trait. And we may state that *Chazal* intended to convey this idea in their dictum (Avoth 1.2), "The world rests on three things: on Torah, on the sacrificial service, and on rendering acts of *chesed*."

We may also assert that the most desirable of all ends is for man to be worthy to remain in God's presence and to enjoy the effulgence of the *Shechina*. This is the true state of bliss, the greatest of all pleasures. Yet whether man merits it depends upon whether he clings to God with all his might while he is still alive, as it is written (Deut. 11.22), "to cling to Him," which means to cling to His attributes.

Chazal have so declared: During all his days, man should urge himself on to acquire the Divine attributes, which are directed to goodness and kindness only. Then he will deserve to remain eternally before God and to "satisfy his soul in drought," as it is written, (Micah 7.18) "since He delights in *chesed*." This would not be true if his attitude in life was: to be opposed to helping his fellow man, to act contrary to the ways of God. How could such a person deserve to be close to God in the end? This is indeed the idea expressed by the *Gemara* (Eruvin 86a): "Rava bar Mari expounded the verse (Ps. 61.8), 'May the world exist before God; kindness (*chesed*) and truth (*emeth*) shall sustain it.' When shall the world endure in the presence of God? — when *chesed* and *emeth* shall protect it *(man yintzeruhu)*. (When there will be generous, wealthy people who provide the poor with food, then they will protect it. *'Man'* referring to food [Rashi].) And Scripture chooses the term *yintzeruhu* (will protect it) advisedly, for the world requires special protection to survive in so holy a region as in the presence of God, where angels and seraphim abound, each of whom, by himself, could destroy the entire world with the breath of his mouth, as we find in *Sifrei, Haazinu*. Special merit, then, is required to avoid destruction by the powers of justice. Hence Scripture states: Whoever possesses the virtues of Torah knowledge (*emeth*) and kindness (*chesed*) will be preserved by them.

Chazal have expressed the same idea (Yerushalmi Ta'anith 4.2): " 'And I have put My words in your mouth' (Isa. 51.16) refers to words of Torah; 'And have covered you with the shadow of my palm' refers to acts of kindness" — the intention being that the kindnesses a person dispenses with his hand make him worthy to be covered by the shadow (protection) of God's 'palm.' From here it is evident that whosoever occupies himself with Torah and lovingkindness will be worthy to survive through Divine protection.

Now everyone can understand how far his love for the virtue of *chesed* should extend. Consequently when he becomes suffused with the love for this virtue, he will react, each time God provides him with the opportunity to perform a deed of kindness, as if he had suddenly found a valuable article. He will perform the deed to perfection. No one borrowing from him would suffer embarrassment. And so God will bless him. Moreover, when a person feels a love for this mitzvah, he will stimulate others to engage in it as well, as Rabbi Yonah (Gerundi) has set down in his *Iggereth Hateshuvah*.

3

ANOTHER REASON FOR THE TORAH URGING
THE PURSUIT OF CHESED

It would also be appropriate for me to elucidate the comment of the *Yalkut* on the verse in Psalm 17, "Let my judgment come forth from Your presence." "Rabbi Levi said: the Holy One, blessed be He, said to David, 'Have you set up a Sanhedrin to no purpose? Let them try you.' David answered Him: 'Master of the universe, You have written down in Your Torah (Exod. 23.8), 'You shall take no bribe,' They (the Sanhedrin) would be afraid to be guilty of accepting bribes when they try me. But You permit Yourself to be bribed, as it is said (Prov. 7.23), 'He shall accept a bribe from the bosom of the wicked.' And what is the bribe? — *teshuvah,* which the Holy One blessed be He receives from the evil-doers in this world, and also good deeds." The Holy One, blessed be He, said to Israel: My sons! Repent, while the gates of *teshuvah* are still open, for I shall accept bribes offered in this world, but not when I shall sit in judgment in the world to come, of which it is said (Prov. 6.35), 'He will not favor the offerer of bribes.' "

It seems strange at first sight. What connection can there be between repentance and good deeds on the one hand and bribery on the other? If repentance should, by right, be ineffective in the world to come, what has this to do with bribery? Is not God the God of truth? The answer is that there are two factors by which God controls the world from above: the *middoth* of justice, and of kindness and compassion. Now, it is known that man's rewards and punishments in the world to come will be determined by the balance of his mitzvoth against the sins he had committed, as *Chazal* have asserted: "If the majority of a man's deeds are righteous, he belongs in the category of *tzaddik;* if iniquitous, he belongs in the category of *rasha'*."

Every intelligent person understands that once God takes His seat on the throne of *justice* during a trial, then even a man whose merits were exceedingly numerous would leave the Heavenly court condemned (unless he had strained with all his might to fulfill all the mitzvoth in all their details). Every one of his mitzvoth would be subjected to meticulous scrutiny to determine whether it had conformed to every requirement of the law. Even what is normally hidden from view (the nature of his mental attitude at the time) would also be most carefully examined for the proper love, awe and joy at its performance, and the other factors required in every mitzvah, which are detailed in the *Sefer Charedim,* and as Scripture declares (Eccl. 12.14): "For God shall bring every work into the judgment concerning what is hidden . . ." Certainly He would find many mitzvoth the requirements of which were not completely fulfilled, and these would be excluded from the account. Then, consequently, the person's iniquities would outnumber his good deeds and he would, God forbid, be designated as *rasha'*, in heaven. Even had he repented of certain sins, his *teshuvah* would be found, under scrutiny, to have been inadequate.

However, if the Holy One, blessed be He, then decided to deal with man in accordance with His attribute of *chesed* and compassion — although it would, certainly, make a great difference whether all the dictates of the mitzvah were obeyed or whether some details were overlooked — nevertheless, some redeeming feature would be found for his improper performance, and his merits would not be rejected. It is even conceivable that a person's iniquities might outnumber his meritorious acts. Yet, if God were to exercise the full measure of His compassion, the sins would be reduced in number.

Assuredly, many of them could be termed unintentional or ascribed to some extenuating circumstance. Then, if these would be deducted from the iniquities, the person's merits would outweigh his faults and the name *tzaddik* would be assigned to him. Certainly, if he had repented of several of his misdeeds, his *teshuvah* would be accepted, imperfect as it may have been.

Of course, every person would like God to treat him with the *middoth* of kindness and compassion. Yet these divine attributes themselves are so exercised that they accord with the principles of justice. In so far as man's conduct in this world exemplifies these characteristics, so does he attract the corresponding attributes towards himself from the Heavenly sources. If, in his dealings with others, he is accustomed to act according to these *middoth,* he calls forth the Divine attributes of mercy, and then God has compassion on the world for his sake. Of necessity, man's soul is fed by the fruits of his conduct. Hence he deserves that God extend the same consideration to him when he stands in need of compassion. As *Chazal* have declared (Shabbath 151b): 'Everyone who has compassion on his fellow creatures is himself granted compassion by Heaven."

So the holy *Zohar* expressed it (Sidrah Emor): "The act below stimulates a corresponding activity above. If a man performs a worthy act on earth, he awakens the corresponding power above. Thus, if a man does kindness on earth, he awakens *chesed* above, and it rests on that day which is crowned therewith through him. Similarly, if he performs a deed of mercy, he crowns that day with mercy, and it becomes his protector in the hour of need . . . giving him measure for measure. Happy is the man who exhibits the proper conduct below, since all depends on his act to awaken the corresponding activity above."

If during his lifetime a person was in the habit of not foregoing anything of his own for another, of not having pity on others, he reinforces the attribute of Heavenly justice. So afterwards, when he is in need of such benefits, he is paid back with his own attitude. God

deals with him with that attribute. This is the idea expressed in Isaiah
(3.10): "Say of the righteous that it will be well with him; for they
shall eat the fruit of their doings. Woe unto the wicked! It shall be ill
with him, for the work of his hands shall be done to him."

Here then is what *Chazal* intended to convey by declaring that the
Holy One, blessed be He, accepts repentance and good deeds and
bribes. "Good deeds" refer to the charity and *chesed* which one dispenses in this world. These acts cause one's repentance to be accepted in Heaven, even if it is inadequate from the point of view of
pure justice. By his good deeds, while still alive, the person has
drawn the Divine attributes of *chesed* and *rachamim* (compassion)
towards himself. And so the very attribute of justice itself will be in-
clined to treat him with *chesed* — to give him full credit in the end for
his repentance and all his mitzvoth.

Now we can appreciate why, throughout the Torah, God, may He
be blessed, pressed man to embody this trait, for as is well known
from Scripture (Micah 7.18), "God desires lovingkindness."
Hashem's desire is that his people be vindicated in their trials in the
time to come and not, God forbid, be declared guilty. Therefore,
many times over in the Torah, He commanded them to follow in all
His ways, the paths of goodness and kindness, so that He will be
able, in the end, to conduct himself towards them in accordance with
this *middah*.

4

MAN ENJOYS THE FRUIT OF THIS MITZVAH IN THIS WORLD; WHILE THE STOCK IS STORED UP FOR THE WORLD TO COME. THE MERIT STANDS BY HIM TO RESCUE HIM FROM ALL TROUBLE

Come! See for yourself how great this mitzvah is. It is one of those mitzvoth, the fruit of which man consumes in this world, while the stock remains in the world to come, as is asserted in the Mishnah (Peah 1.1). *Chazal* (*Yerushalmi* ibid.) adds that *chesed* stands by man until the end of all generations, as Scripture (Ps. 103.17) states: "And the *chesed* of God endures for ever and ever for those that fear Him." The effect of charity on the other hand lasts only for three generations, as we find (ibid.), "And His charity for the sons of sons." Now, acts of lovingkindness are designated as the "*chesed* of God" because, through them, we cause God to exercise this Divine attribute, as we have previously asserted in Chapter 3.

Its merit also stands by man in his hour of need and rescues him from his troubles, as we find in *Avodah Zarah* (17b): "Our Rabbis taught: When R. El'azar b. Perata and R. Chanina b. Teradion were arrested, R. El'azar said to R. Chanina: Happy are you! You have been arrested on one charge. Woe is me! I have been arrested on five charges. R. Chanina replied: Happy are you! You have been arrested on five charges, but you will go free. Woe is me! Though I have been arrested on one charge, I shall not go free. You occupied yourself with the study of Torah as well as with acts of *chesed*, whereas I occupied myself with Torah study alone. This accords with the view of R. Huna. For R. Huna said: "He who only occupies himself with Torah study is as if he had no God, for it is said (2 Chr. 15.3): 'Now for long seasons Israel was without the true God.' What is meant by 'without the true God'? — It means that he who only occupies himself with the study of Torah is as if he had no God to protect him." (See Rashi ibid.) Take note of what the *Gemara* (ibid.) states. R. Chanina as well occupied himself with acts of kindness. He was a charity treasurer. Yet he did not do as much as he should.

The content of this passage can be further elucidated by an excerpt from the Midrash (Ruth Rabba Chap. 5): "Come and consider how great is the power of those who perform acts of charity, how great is the power of those who do kindly deeds (*chesed*), for they shelter neither in the shadow of the morning, nor in the shadow of the wings of the earth, nor in the shadow of the sun, nor in the shadow of the wings of the chayoth or the cherubim or the seraphim, but under whose wings do they shelter? — Under the shadow of Him at Whose word the world was created, as it is said (Ps. 36.8): 'How precious is Your lovingkindness, O God! And the children of man take refuge under the shadow of Your wings.' " This is what the passage intends to convey: When the Heavenly tribunal conducts a trial, there are many angels of mercy among the Sanhedrin (in fact, they form a majority and stand at the right side of the Divine throne to seek merit for the person judged — they are called *nedivim* according to the *Sha'arei Orah*). Nevertheless, they, too, act in accord with justice. When the Holy One, blessed be He, sits in judgment by Himself, however, then pure mercy holds sway. Hence Scripture asserts (Ps. 118.8): "It is better to trust in God than to trust in *nedivim*." God, however, conducts the trial on His own only when the person judged has acted with kindness, and has thereby opened up the Heavenly sources of *chesed* for himself. Only then does he merit having the Holy One, blessed be He, as his sole Judge. This is what the Midrash (Ruth Rabba 5.4) meant to say: "Come and consider how great is the power of the charitable, how great is the power of those who do kindly deeds . . .as it is said (Ps. 36.8): 'How precious is Your lovingkindness, O God. . .' "How precious, indeed, it is when the children of men awaken Your *chesed* and so become worthy of the protection of "the shadow of Your wings" and not the wings of others.

The same idea is expressed in the Psalms (17.2): "Let my judgment come forth from Your presence; let Your eyes behold the right," i.e. from Your presence alone, and not with the participation of the Heavenly court. So too it is written (2 Chr. 18.18): "I saw God sitting on His throne and all the host of heaven standing on His right hand and on His left" — on the right to acquit and on the left to convict, as *Chazal* have explained. The distinction referred to above is brought out by the conclusion of the verse: "Let Your eyes behold the right" — meaning that when God himself will focus his mercies upon the just and the perverse, He will seek some merit, perhaps some fortuitous circumstance that provoked the evil deed. Not so when the whole Heavenly court sits in judgment. Certainly the person brought to trial cannot hope to gain acquittal in such a case.

Now we can understand the passage in question. If man occupies himself with the study of Torah and acts of kindness and so awakens the Divine attribute of mercy, then when he is, God forbid, in trouble, the Holy One, blessed be He, Himself, will hear his case and extend His *chesed* to him. So the person will surely be saved. It is otherwise when a person has been exclusively preoccupied with Torah study, and did not devote himself sufficiently to acts of *chesed*. Then the Heavenly *chesed* is correspondingly not aroused on his behalf. So if he afterwards suffers distress, God forbid, and he is, at the same time, arraigned in Heaven, then he will not succeed in entirely preventing the forces of justice exercising power over him. This is the meaning of *Chazal's* assertion: "He who only occupies himself with Torah study and not with kindness is as if he has no God." He is like one who has no God to shield him by His Divine mercies and *chesed* from the forces of justice, because he had cast those holy virtues behind him.

A similar idea is expressed in *Bava Kamma* (17a), according to one version: "Whoever occupies himself with Torah and acts of *chesed*, his enemies shall fall before him, as is written of Joseph (Deut. 33.17): 'He shall gore the people, all of them, even to the ends of the earth.' He acquires intuitive understanding like the children of Issachar, of whom it is written (1 Chr. 12.32): 'And the children of Issachar that had understanding of the times...' " Through the merit of Torah study one acquires understanding like the children of Issachar, whose occupation was Torah and thereby they acquired understanding; through his acts of *chesed* one causes his enemies to fall before him, as Joseph did because he engaged in acts of kindness in very great measure. He supplied food to many lands during the famine, and in particular to his father Jacob's family. Also he took care of his father's funeral, and this too is deemed *chesed* by Scripture (Gen. 47.29), "Deal kindly (with *chesed*) and truly with me."

From all that has been said, one should appreciate the greatness of the virtue of *chesed*; one should cling to it, as so be rescued from distress both in this world and the next.

5

THE GREATNESS AND OTHER ASPECTS OF THE REWARD ACQUIRED THROUGH THIS MITZVAH

How closely must one cling to the virtue of *chesed!* It is effective in awakening Divine mercies and *chesed* for Israel even after the merit accumulated by the forefathers has been exhausted. As *Chazal* have said (*Yerushalmi Sanhedrin* 10.1): "R. Yudah b. Chanan in the name of R. Berechya: God said to Israel: My children, if you see the merit of the patriarchs and matriarchs faltering, go and engage in acts of kindness. What is the reason? — 'For the mountains may depart and the hills falter' (Isa. 54.10) — 'for the mountains may depart' refers to the patriarchs; 'and the hills may falter' refers to the matriarchs. From here onwards 'My kindness shall not depart from you ... says God that has compassion on you.' " This passage teaches us the following idea: Our father Abraham extended only goodness and kindness to all the world, as is shown by his good deeds recorded in the *sidrah, Vayerah.* The same behavior was characteristic of the rest of the patriarchs, as we find (Gen 18.19): "For I have known him to the end that he may command his children and his household after him that they may keep the way of God to do righteousness and justice." Hence, they caused God's *chesed* to become manifest over all His creatures. Prior to the patriarchs, the Shechinah was confined to the seventh firmament. Through their holy deeds, the forefathers drew the glory of God down to the world, where it has remained, because of them. So the Midrash has it: "Abraham came and brought it to the sixth, Isaac to

94

the fifth . . .until, at the time of the revelation at Mt. Sinai, the Shechinah came down to earth."

Now since man is obviously confined within time and space, his deeds cannot penetrate beyond a certain limit — the furthest point his merit can reach. Hence Scripture has advised us that when we see the merits of our forefathers becoming exhausted, we should ourselves awaken the attributes of God's goodness and *chesed* for us, by clinging in our deeds to these same virtues. Then, measure for measure, His *chesed* will envelop us and will never depart from us. (The expression *lo yamush* carries the implication of "will *never* depart", as in the verse Exod. 13.22, *lo yamish* — "the pillar of cloud shall *not at any time* depart.")

This mitzvah also contributes to the deliverance of Israel from among the gentile nations, as is shown in *Berachoth* 8a. In importance it exceeds the sacrificial service, as is borne out by the *Yalkut's* (Hosea 522) comment on the verse (Ibid. 6.6): " 'For I desire kindness and not sacrifice' — The Holy one, blessed be He, declared: "The kindnesses you extend to each other are more precious to Me than all the sacrifices offered by King Solomon' " ["A thousand burnt offerings did Solomon bring" (1 Kings 3.41)].

The lesson has been even more emphatically expressed in the *Yerushalmi* (*Peah* 1.1): "*Peah,* charity, and acts of *chesed* are equal in importance to all the rest of the mitzvoth of the Torah." The Midrash declares (Ruth Rabba 2.14): "R. Zeira said: The scroll (of Ruth) tells us nothing of ritual purity or impurity, or prohibition or permission. For what purpose was it written? — To teach how great is the reward of those who do deeds of kindness." This passage refers to Boaz, who earned the merit of being the progenitor of David. And for David and his children, royalty was reserved for them forever.

Rains, too are vouchsafed for the merit of *chesed,* as the *Yerushalmi Ta'anith* points out. Through it, too, one condemned to die by act of God, Heaven forbid, is delivered from his fate (*Tanchuma*

Kedoshim). It is also effective in rescuing man from the clutches
of his evil desires, as we find (*Avodah Zarah* 5b): "Blessed is Israel.
When they occupy themselves with Torah and *gemiluth chesed*
their inclination is mastered by them, not they by their inclination,
as it is said (Isa. 32.20): 'Blessed are you that sow beside all waters.'" What is meant here is that man's inclination strives to
master him in two ways. Firstly, it attempts to divert his attention to
foolish matters, and secondly, to habituate his limbs to all manner of
activity contrary to the will of God, may He be blessed. However,
whoever occupies himself with Torah and with acts of kindness succeeds in subduing his inclinations and in bringing them under his
control. Through Torah, one is occupied with the teachings of the
living God, and so he sanctifies his intellectual powers; while,
through acts of kindness, he sanctifies his bodily organs, since these
are now taken up with the service of the King of the Universe. So we
find (Exod. 10.12, 11.22): "To walk in all His ways" — and (Exod.
18.12): "And you shall make known to them the way in which they
shall go," which refers to all the ways of goodness of the Holy One,
blessed be He. So *Chazal* have asserted. Man thereby acquires im-
munity to the enticements of his inclinations to do the opposite.

Whoever, then, performs this mitzvah consistently earns the merit
of having children who are wise, wealthy and versed in the Aggadah — in the words of *Chazal* (*Bava Bathra* 9b): "R. Yehoshua b.
Levi said: He who does charity habitually shall have sons, wise,
wealthy and versed in the Aggadah — 'Wise' as it is written (Prov.
21.21): 'Whosoever pursues charity shall find life' (and regarding
wisdom, Scripture states [Prov. 8.35]: 'Who finds me finds
life'—Rashi); 'wealthy'—as it is written (Ibid. 21.21): 'He shall find
prosperity'; versed in the Aggadah — as it is written (Prov. 3.35):
'The wise shall inherit honor' (i.e. their popular homiletical exposi-
tions of the Torah will attract large audiences, and all will honor
them — Rashi). Now R. Yehoshua spoke of "charity", but his
remarks apply equally to *chesed* as well, for the verse quoted

declares: "Whoever pursues charity and *kindness*." The reason that he confined his comment to "charity" was to convey that the reward of "life, prosperity and honor" is granted for each virtue separately, and not only for the two together.

All the blessings of the Torah possess this characteristic, as we find in connection with the verse (Deut. 28.22): "And all these blessings shall come upon you and overtake you if you will hearken to the voice of *Hashem*, your God." The *Tanna debei Eliyahu* (end of Chap. 26) comments: "When will all these blessings come upon you? – If you will obey *Hashem*, your God, and walk in His ways, the ways of Heaven. What are the ways of Heaven? – As He is merciful, as He has compassion even on the wicked and receives them when they repent wholeheartedly, and as He feeds and sustains all creatures – so shall you be merciful to one another, support one another, be gracious to one another. Another explanation: What are the ways of Heaven? – He is gracious and gives His bounty as a free gift both to those who know Him and to those who do not. So shall you give free gifts to one another. Yet another explanation: What are the ways of Heaven? – He dispenses *chesed* in abundance, and inclines his acts towards *chesed*; so shall you favor one another, grant charity to one another and incline towards goodness . . .

From all that has been said, one can gain an impression of the greatness of the virtue of *chesed*. Happy is the person who clings to it wholeheartedly, since he acquires merit for the coming generations.

6

THE SUBJECT FURTHER EXPLAINED

Come and see how great a reward is given to the one who is kind to his fellow men! Even the indirect consequences of his acts are credited to him just as if he had performed them himself. This takes many forms, as we shall, to some extent, explain and thereby demonstrate the importance of the subject.

(1) As affects the person himself: Suppose one was kind to some suffering, ailing individual. Through the kind man's financial help the sufferer's health was restored. Then, in the assessment of the kind man's reward, not only are the few silver coins he spent taken into account, but he is considered actually to have restored the sufferer's life to him. The evidence of such a conclusion lies in the words of *Chazal (Tanchuma Mishpatim* 15): "So began R. Tanchuma: 'He that is gracious to the poor lends to God, and his good deeds He will |re|pay him' (Prov. 19.17). The one who lends to the poor is as it were, lending money to God, and He will give him his recompense. R. Pinchas the Kohen b. Chama said in the name of R. Reuven: What does 'and will repay him' convey?—One may think that if a person gave a penny to a poor man, God will give him a penny in return. Instead, God says: The poor man was in the throes of death brought on by hunger. You nourished and revived him. By your life! I shall restore a life to you in return. Tomorrow your son or your daughter may be near illness or death. I shall remember what you did for the poor man, and shall save them from death for your sake. This is 'and will repay him'—God will repay a life for a

98

life." Another important lesson is contained in this verse. A person may need a specific favor or a courtesy. God will repay him according to his deeds. If his nature is to have pity on and to be gracious to others, he too will receive favor and people will be good to him. If the contrary is true, Heaven forbid, God will give him his deserts. This is what Scripture teaches by: "He that is gracious to the poor lends to God, and his good deeds He will [re]pay him."

(2) All the benefits accruing to others as a result of his deed will be credited to him. Suppose, for instance, someone had lost his possessions. Then this person lent him a sum of money. The recipient employed the money profitably and was able to support his family and himself. He also, in effect, provided food and drink for his employees. Here the benefactor is regarded as having helped all who benefitted from the business, since the entire enterprise developed out of his original act. We find such an incident described by *Chazal* (Bava Kamma 9a): "R. Yochanan said: To rob a fellow man even of the value of a *perutah* is like taking his life away, as it says (Prov. 1.19): 'So are the ways of everyone that is greedy of gain, which takes away the life of the owners thereof.' You might think that this refers only to his life, but not to the lives of his sons and his daughters, so Scripture says (Jer. 5.17): 'And he shall eat up your harvest and your bread which your sons and daughters should eat.' You might say that this applies to the case when he committed the act directly, but not when he was the indirect cause of the robbery. Come and consider (1 Sam. 21.1): 'It is for Saul and his bloody house because he put the Gibeonites to death.' Where does it say that Saul slew the Gibeonites?—It must therefore be because he slew Nob and the city of priests who used to supply them with food and drink (in payment for the wood and water which the Gibeonites hewed and drew for the altar) that Scripture considers him to have slain them." Here we see how Divine justice is administered—how awesome it is, since all the consequences of man's actions are taken into consideration, even where his deeds have only indirectly caused

harm to his neighbors. He need not have been the direct cause of harm. He need only have indirectly prevented a person from providing the gainful occupation from which his neighbor could earn the means to support his household. Yet Heaven considers him actually to have taken the life of the person and his household; therefore a grave punishment is meted out to him.

It is well known that the measure of God's beneficence exceeds the measure of His punishment. Punishment lasts to the third and fourth generation; while of beneficence it is written (Exod. 21.6): "And doing kindness to the thousandth generation" as *Chazal* have explained (Tosefta Sotah Chap. 4). How much greater, then, is the effect if, in a specific instance, one does his neighbor a favor and through it accrues benefit to the neighbor's household and to others as well. Whatever good results from his act will be added to his credit when he is to receive his reward. Once man reflects on this, he will strive to help his neighbor in every way possible.

We should also consider: How can one lift up his face to the Holy One, blessed be He, and ask, "Grant peace, welfare, blessing, grace, lovingkindness and mercy to us . . .", if he has no desire to deal with his neighbor in compassion or kindness. God would hardly accept his many requests if he himself does not practice *chesed*. This is especially true of the many petitions for daily sustenance which one constantly addresses to *Hashem*, may He be blessed, where one is entirely dependent on the *chesed* of the Holy One — as we recite in our daily prayers: "Who sustains life in kindness." When a person has habitually practised the virtue of kindness, however, his petitions will surely be accepted by God, may He be blessed, and his requests will be granted. So *Chazal* have asserted (*Midrash Shocher Tov* Chap. 65): "As for Ben Azzai and R. Akiva, one of them declared: Whoever bestows lovingkindness will receive the good tidings that his *Tefillah* has been accepted, as it is said (Hos. 10.12): 'Sow to yourselves according to righteousness, reap according to lovingkindness.' What is written next? — 'It is time to seek God.' He prays to God and is answered; he receives the glad tidings that his request has been fulfilled. And Chanina said: I do not dispute the statement of my master, but come to add to it: 'As for me, in the abundance of Your lovingkindness will I come into Your house' (Ps. 5.8). Immediately afterwards it says (Ps. 69.14): 'You answer me with Your salvation.'"

Our discussion so far refers to extending *chesed* to an ordinary Jew; how much more necessary is it to lend a *Talmid Chacham* sums sufficient for his support. Then the merit of the giver is certainly great. For, through his assistance, the *Talmid Chacham* is free to devote himself to Torah study and, as we have shown, these consequences will be credited to the giver's account. He will be worthy to sit among the *Chachamim* in the Heavenly Academy. *Chazal* have expressed the idea in these terms (Pesachim 53b): "R. Yochanan said: Whoever casts merchandise into the pockets of *chachamim* will be privileged to sit in the Heavenly Academy, for it is said (Eccl. 7.12): 'For wisdom is defence even as money is defence.'" ('Whoever casts merchandise'—to enable the *Chacham* to engage in trade. 'Wisdom is defence'—the giver will enter the area reserved for *Chachamim*, since he allowed them the use of his possessions [Rashi].) (This statement does not apply only to merchandise but to any similar benefit through which a *Talmid Chacham* may become self supporting. Merchandise is mentioned here because, in earlier generations, it was customary to supply wares to the *Talmid Chacham* at cost, so that he could sell them and support himself out of the profits.) On the verse (Deut. 4.4): "But you who cleave to *Hashem* your God are alive every one of you this day," the *Gemara* (Kethuvoth 112a) comments: "Is it really possible to cleave to the Shechinah?—Is it not written (Ibid. v. 24): '*Hashem* your God is a devouring fire?' The meaning is: Whoever gives his daughter in marriage to a *Talmid Chacham* and whoever engages in business on behalf of a *Talmid Chacham* (he invests the latter's money so that the scholar receives an income and is free to occupy himself with

Torah study [Rashi]), and whoever gives the benefit of his property to a *Talmid Chacham* is regarded by Scripture as if 'he cleaves to the *Shechinah.*' " (See Chap. 26 where we have quoted other Rabbinic literature dealing with the greatness of the reward for such behavior.)

7

THE GREATNESS OF THE HARM RESULTING FROM WITHHOLDING CHARITY AND CHESED

In the previous chapters we have elucidated the greatness of this holy virtue. Now we shall expose the evil nature of the person who avoids it, who shuts his eyes to it. We have learned (Kethuvoth 68a): "Anyone who shuts his eyes against charity is like one who worships idols, for it is written (Deut. 15.9): 'Beware that there be not a base thought (*beli-ya'al*) in your heart . . . and your eye will be evil against your brother,' and there (concerning the city where the inhabitants were guilty of idolatry—Tr.) it is written (Ibid. 13.14): 'Certain base fellows (*beli-ya'al*) have gone out.' " (The inference is drawn by *Gezerah Shavah*—Tr.). Now it is known that the verse (Deut. 15.9) also refers to a person refusing a request for a loan, as we find in *Gittin* 37a and *Sotah* 47b. Now let each person consider: Suppose someone called him '*Beli-Ya'al*'. How much resentment would he harbor against the person who insulted him, even if the two of them had been alone at the time, and he therefore suffered no public embarrassment. How angry should a person be with himself, then, if he causes the *Torah* to call him by this name! How much shame and humiliation will ultimately attach to him in Heaven!

He should also be apprehensive because perhaps the person he wronged will cry out against him, as it is written (Deut. 15.9): "And he cry out against you to God and it shall be a sin in you." One's entire situation might be changed, as *Chazal* have indicated (Temurah 16a): "When a poor man approaches a rich man and cries 'Help me!' (i.e. prevent my falling by giving me a gift or a loan to make me self-supporting. [See Betzah 32a]), if he assists him it is well, but if not (Prov. 22.2) 'the rich and the poor meet together and God is Master of them all.' He who made this one rich can make him poor, and He who made the other poor can make him rich."

It is also evident from literature that the sin of withholding charity or *chesed* from a fellow Jew causes one's possessions eventually to pass into the hands of others, he himself being left naked and bare. The verse (Deut. 28.47) expresses the idea thus: "Because you did not serve *Hashem*, your God, with joyfulness and gladness of heart when you had an abundance, you shall serve your enemy whom God shall send against you in hunger, in thirst, in nakedness and in want of all things . . ." And *Tanna debei Eliyahu* (Chap. 16) comments: "How shall they suffer hunger?—When the poor man approaches the rich and begs a drop of beer or cider to drink, and the rich refuses it, idol-worshippers come and demand the world's best wine from him. 'Nakedness and want?'—When the poor approaches the rich for a linen or woollen tunic to wear, and the rich man does not give him one, then idol-worshippers come and demand his most elegant silks." The rule applies to *chesed* as well. Suppose a certain person did not want to serve God joyfully. He did not extend the kindness to his fellow Jew that befitted his means and through which he would have fulfilled the positive Torah commandment (Exod. 22.24): "When you lend money . . ." Had he behaved properly his money would have eventually come back to him. Now he will, inevitably, lose many times that sum to strangers and he will be powerless to recover it from them. Even if a person does give some charity and performs some *chesed* with his money, but not in accordance with his means, then his money may become forfeited as a result. A curse will become attached to it. If others engage in a business venture with him, their capital will be lost because of him. (See Kethuvoth 66b/67a concerning the dwindling of Nakdimon ben Gurion's daughter's wealth).

For withholding charity and kindness he will be among those condemned to *Gehennom*. So the *Gemara* (Betzah 32b) bears out: "Rav said: The rich of Babylon will go down to *Gehennom*." Their sin, as related there, was that they refused to perform acts of charity and kindness. In *Vayikra Rabba* (34.12) we find: "R. Yehudah and R. Shimon in the name of R. Yehoshua b. Levi: Let the mitzvah of helping the poor never appear trivial in your eyes—for its nonperformance evokes 24 curses, while its performance earns 24 blessings. From where do we deduce 24 curses?—As it is said (Ps. 109.6): 'Set a wicked man over him . . .,' and why all this?—Because he did not remember to engage in *chesed*. And the reward is 24 blessings, as it is written (Isa. 58.7): 'Is it not to deal your bread to the hungry . . . Then shall you delight yourself in God and I will make you ride on the high places of the earth." (The Midrashic commentators [ad loc.] explain how the number is arrived at—Tr.) Also, by refraining from giving charity and acting benevolently, one causes God to withdraw His peace from Israel, as is mentioned in this connection (Bava Bathra 10a): "As it says (Jer. 16.5): 'Thus says God: Enter not into the house of mourning, neither go to lament, neither bemoan them, for I have taken away my peace from this people, says God, even lovingkindness and tender mercies.' 'Lovingkindness' refers to *gemiluth chesed*, 'tender mercies' to charity," (which they used to perform, but do so no more [Rashi]).

On the verse (Deut. 23.5): Because they (Ammon and Moab) met you not with bread and water . . .," *Vayikra Rabba* (34) comments: "Did Israel need their favors? Did not manna come down, water gush forth, the quail fly, the cloud of glory surround them and the pillar of cloud travel ahead of them during all the forty years?—But this is common courtesy: When a wayfarer passes by, he should be greeted with food and drink. How did God repay them their deserts? He forbade an Ammonite or a Moabite to enter God's community" (i.e. no male descended paternally from an Ammonite or Moabite proselyte may marry a woman of legitimate Jewish descent—Tr.).

Here we may infer from the lighter to the graver case (*Kal Vachomer*), that if one who refused to be kind to a person who did not need his favor was repaid with such severity, how much more so will a person be punished if he failed to extend kindness to a person who did need his favor!

Consider how great was the shame of the individual who was suspected by *Chazal* (Betzah 32b) of being descended from the "mixed multitude" (Exod. 12.38). "Shabtai b. Marinus came to Babylon, and entreated them to provide him with a loan for trading. (He would share the profits equally with them.) They refused this to him; neither did they give him any food. He said: These are the descendants of the mixed multitude, for it is written (Deut. 13.18): 'And He will show mercy and have compassion upon you.' Whoever is merciful to his fellow men is certainly of the children of our father, Abraham, and whoever is not merciful to his fellow men is certainly not of the children of our father Abraham" (ibid.). And *Chazal* have further declared (Yevamoth 79a): "This nation is distinguished by three characteristics: They are shy, compassionate, and benevolent (*Gomlei chasadim*)." Whoever does not have these three characteristics is not worthy to become part of this nation.

Indeed many other Biblical verses and Rabbinic literature explicitly affirm this rule. However, wishing to be brief, I shall confine myself to a single, all-inclusive passage. Consider how far *Chazal* have gone in describing the wickedness of a person who refrains from performing acts of *chesed*, in saying (Koheleth Rabba 7.1): "If one repudiates his obligation to do *chesed*, it is as though he repudiates the cardinal doctrine (of God's existence)." By this remark they intend to convey that *Hashem*, may He be blessed, is the source of all goodness and kindness. His purpose in all that He created was to give His creatures the opportunity to earn merit, enabling Him to repay them, ultimately, with goodness and kindness. To this end the Torah was revealed and its commandments ordained. As Scripture states (Deut. 6.24): "And God commanded us to do all

these statutes, to fear *Hashem*, our God, for our good always . . ."
Hence if one refuses to accept this view of the virtue of *chesed* and
asks, "What do I need it for?"—his rejection is tantamount to denying the fundamental principle (of God's existence), Heaven forbid.
Hence one should completely avoid such thoughts. He should take
care to cling to the ways of God, may He be blessed, which are
permeated with goodness and kindness, in order to receive goodness
in this world and in the next.

8

WHY PEOPLE ARE NEGLIGENT IN PERFORMING
THIS MITZVAH, AND THE REFUTATION
OF THEIR ARGUMENTS

In the previous chapters we have elaborated on the great reward earned by the person embodying this trait. Now we shall proceed to examine the reasons why people are negligent in the performance of this mitzvah. We shall also demonstrate the fallacies in their arguments. Perhaps people might learn to mend their ways to some extent. I shall begin by pointing out that there are five causes preventing the performance of acts of *chesed*: Fear, ignorance, illusions of being exempt, parsimony and indolence. We shall, with God's help, discuss one by one.

FEAR. Some people are afraid that the debtor will not repay the loan. They are unwilling to accept any security. Yet one should earnestly reflect before he releases himself from this obligation. Firstly, if the amount is small he would, regardless, be bound to give the money to this man as charity, or in fulfillment of the mitzvah (Lev. 25.35): "If your brother becomes poor and his means fail with you, then you shall uphold him." So he certainly is duty bound to *lend* the money, even if there is some danger of financial loss. Even if the sum would not be returned to him, he would still have to give it to the person for the reasons we have mentioned above. And even if these reasons could not be applied in a specific case, as where the amount exceeds what he is obliged to give to charity, or where the mitzvah of "You shall uphold him" is not involved—once the borrower offers him reliable security, he can no longer free himself from the obligation to accept the pledge (unless the borrower is a violent person who could force him to return the article before the loan is repaid).

There is another argument motivated by fear. The person approached is concerned that he himself might need the money at short notice. This argument has some validity. If he needs the money for his household expenses, he certainly takes priority, for his own life comes before his neighbor's. He is also justified where an investment is immediately available, or where he has been approached to give the free loan for a long term, since in this case it is normal for some investment opportunity to present itself during a longer period of time. Still, for someone to refrain from granting a short term loan to the needy while his money lies idle, on the chance that some profitable transaction might suddenly arise, is not a reasonable excuse, unless the person really expects to engage in some enterprise in the near future, and he could not do so without this money. Take note, however, that these considerations apply to a person who is not especially wealthy. He expects the business investment to yield him a living for his household. A really rich person, however, who possesses idle cash, is certainly duty bound to make the loan if the person requesting it is trustworthy or prepared to offer security, even if this loan would preclude him from investing this sum in other business interests. The positive commandment of "When you lend money to the poor" devolves upon everyone in proportion to his means (*Sefer Hachinuch*, Mitzvah 66). In this instance, his means are certainly sufficient. The principle of his life taking precedence over his neighbor's certainly does not apply. This rich man would only use his money to increase his wealth still further, while the borrower would use it for his basic necessities. If the rich man's argument is sustained, there would never be a limit. He could always keep on acquiring new business interests. No amount of investment capital would ever be sufficient for him. He would forever be exempt from the mitzvah of lending to the poor.

There is a third reason, also motivated by fear, for a person refraining from performing the mitzvah of *gemiluth chesed*. He is apprehensive that the public will become aware of his wealth. He would then be subjected to pressure to contribute to communal needs. This contention is certainly groundless. Shall one be absolved from his duty to observe a positive commandment of the Torah because of this fear? This contention has no more validity than the argument of the person who refrains from giving charity for he is afraid of losing his money. In the present case, many Biblical verses and Rabbinic literature indicate that the sin is grave, and the punishment is the loss of one's property in this world, as is evident from the *Gemara* (Kethuvoth 66b). *Tanna debei Eliyahu Zuta* (Chap. 4) declares: "If you have given charity, you will acquire possessions. If you have acquired possessions, give them as charity while they are still in your hands. Buy this world with them, and you shall inherit the world to come. For if you do not use them for charity, they will soon depart, as it is said (Prov. 23.5): 'Shall your eye make it fly away and be gone?' "

One must trust that by obeying God's will with one's money, one will suffer no harm. Instead, one's possessions will be blessed with increase, as it is said (Deut. 5.10): "You shall surely give him and your heart shall not be grieved when you give him, for because of this *Hashem*, your God, will bless you in all your work." What is true of charity is true of *chesed*, as we have shown in our previous chapters. So even if one did gain the reputation of being wealthy, and his communal assessments were therefore increased by a certain amount each year, he should not be swayed by such a consideration, for God will surely repay the damage he suffered in performing the mitzvah. Besides, consider this situation: A person became aware of an investment which would yield him thousands of dollars per year. As a result, however, he would gain the reputation of being rich, and his annual communal assessments and the like would be increased by several dollars. Would he forego the investment so as to appear less affluent and thereby escape the increase in his contributions? If he did, everyone would consider him a fool. This is how such arguments appear in our case. Is it worthwhile to forfeit eternal life for the sake of a few grains of silver? Eternal life is earned thereby, because every time one makes such a loan to his neighbor he fulfills a positive Torah commandment, and the reward for mitzvoth is infinite. The lender will be worthy to shelter in the "wings" of the Holy One, blessed be He, in the world to come, as *Chazal* have declared.

There is another way of meeting this argument of the evil inclination. It is possible for the rich person to deposit his *gemiluth chesed* money in the care of a reliable agent who would conceal the owner's identity. The agent would then allocate the loans on his behalf. This is a matter of great importance, as we shall explain, with God's help, further on, in Chapter 14.

9

THE REFUTATION OF THE RATIONALIZATIONS OF IGNORANCE AND OF THE ARGUMENTS FOR EXEMPTION

IGNORANCE. Some people are negligent in *gemiluth chesed* because of sheer ignorance. They are unaware of the important and obligatory nature of the mitzvah and do not realize the reward it carries. They consider it to be a good trait and commendable conduct, but fail to realize that it is as much a positive command of the Torah as *Sukkah, Lulav and Tefillin.* See, my friend, how we are remiss in this mitzvah. How much effort does every Jew exert in building a Sukkah, in purchasing a Lulav and the like! He is anxious to fulfill all the requirements of the law. He does not afterwards regret, God forbid, his exertions in carrying out God's command. On the contrary, he rejoices that God gave him the opportunity to exert himself to perform these mitzvoth, and that he was able to fulfill them. (So should we indeed rejoice when we reflect that man is, after all, a small creature whose days are numbered and who is destined to become dust and ashes, and yet he stands on the earth and is worthy to serve *Hashem*, God of the heavens, just like one of the heavenly hosts.) On the other hand, how grudgingly do we look down on *gemiluth chesed*! Even a small inconvenience is sufficient for us to avoid its performance. And when we do act, it is with reluctance and sadness, without a trace of pleasure.

I shall describe a single case, and an intelligent person can apply it to similar situations. Suppose one person meets another in the street, and says to him: "Brother, would you lend me a few dollars for a short time?" Even if the latter considers the person seeking the loan reliable, he will find a thousand reasons for turning down the request. Sometimes he will answer that it is too much effort for him to go home to get the money; the borrower should have come at another time, and to him at home. Or else he might tell him that he only has a ten dollar bill with him and is unwilling to break it, or else he might suggest that he go and borrow from somebody else —or any of many similar excuses. If the poor man pleads with him, and he finally goes home or changes the bill and lends the borrower the money, he does so reluctantly and sadly, without a trace of joy. His facial expression is soured by the trouble to which he was put.

Now, consider, my friend! Suppose a man whom you held to be reliable met you in the street and said: "Quickly, brother, go to your home. I have a good business proposition to tell you about. The down payment is small . . . but you'll profit well. After the transaction is completed, you may give me a modest sum for my recommendation." Would you tell such a person: "I'm too tired to go back home or [to obtain a certified check]. Go to that other person. He will take up the deal." No, you would rush home immediately and find ways and means to secure the investment for yourself. And once you saw that the venture was brought to a successful conclusion, how warmly would you praise the person for giving you the good advice!

So indeed is our case. When someone approaches you for a free loan, the transaction is a minor one as far as the recipient, the borrower himself, is concerned. He will gain a few pieces of silver through it. You, the lender, on the other hand, the bestower of kindness, have been approached to engage in a major undertaking involving a positive commandment of the Torah, the reward for which is eternal. You should have rejoiced. You should have received this person in a happy frame of mind. And if God, may He be blessed, has helped you so that you have the ability to act benevolently, you should have rushed to perform this mitzvah, as Scripture puts it (Prov. 21.21): "Whoever pursues charity and *chesed* shall find life, prosperity and honor." (*Chazal* have pointed out that the receiver benefits the giver more than the giver benefits the receiver.) Only because of our many sins is the evil inclination able to minimize the importance of this mitzvah in our eyes—to have us regard it as merely a commendable habit. The recommended remedy for correcting such an attitude is to study the relevant passages in the Codes clarifying the subject. One should also meditate on the Aggadoth of *Chazal* which set forth its significance and the details of its reward for us. In this way, the *yetzer harah* will be overcome.

THE ILLUSION THAT ONE IS EXEMPT. Others consider themselves exempt. They argue with their conscience: "Am I the only one in the whole city? Let him go to those others. They are richer than I." This argument is fallacious. Firstly, who knows whether they will be willing to help? *Radbaz* has recorded in his responsa that, if a person has rich relatives who are unwilling to help him, the rest of the inhabitants of the city are obliged to. If his relatives deviate from God's laws, is he therefore to die of hunger? Furthermore, since the person originally approached has the means, he is not absolved from the positive commandment just because there happen to be richer men than he in the city. What we have written before also provides a logical refutation of this argument.

On some occasions, a person considers himself released from the mitzvah because he had previously lent money to someone else, and the latter had failed to repay him. This, too, is not a logical argument. If some person has proved himself wicked, a borrower who fails to repay his debts, have all Israel thereby been proved bad risks? No! As long as one recognizes a person as a safe risk, he is not absolved from his duty to lend him the money, since he does possess the means—especially where the borrower is willing to furnish security for the loan. As for the borrower who failed to repay him, there are two possibilities in his case. If he was negligent because he is a person of power and arbitrarily withholds the money, then possibly one is not bound to lend him money ever again, even were he to offer a pledge as security, since he might later bring the lender to court on a false charge (and so regain his pledge without repaying the loan). On the other hand, if the debtor was not able to repay—he had, for instance, become impoverished—then the lender would not be released if, this time, the borrower furnishes a pledge.

10

THE EVIL TRAIT OF BEING PARSIMONIOUS

PARSIMONY. Some people avoid this mitzvah out of niggardliness (they begrudge others the use of their money). *Chazal* have already declared (Sotah 47b): "When the niggardly and plunderers of the poor multiplied, those who hardened their hearts and closed their hands against lending to the poor also increased, and they transgressed what is written in the Torah (Deut. 15.9): 'Beware that there be not a base thought in your heart...'"

This is a very ugly trait. It leads one to refrain from giving charity and performing acts of *chesed*. It causes one to repress all feelings of pity and compassion—to stop up one's ears and to be deaf to the cry of the poor.

Sometimes such conduct can even lead to bloodshed. So we find (Sotah 38b): "R. Yehoshua b. Levi said: The heifer whose neck has to be broken is only brought on account of niggardliness of spirit, as it is said (Deut. 21.7): 'Our hands have not shed this blood.' Now can it enter our minds that the elders of a Court of Justice are shedders of blood! The meaning is that the man found dead did not come to us for help and we dismissed him; we did not see him and let him go, i.e. he did not come to us for help and we dismissed him without supplying him with food; we did not see him and let him go without support (i.e. he needed food and could not obtain any. Seeing someone carrying food, he was driven by his hunger to snatch it from him. Thereupon, the other retaliated and killed him. [Rashi])." So we see that if a person approached his neighbor for some help

116

and, because of this wicked trait of parsimony, the latter paid no attention to him, and the needy one died as a result, the Torah
proclaims the refuser a shedder of blood.

Chazal have denounced this evil characteristic and have declared
(Ibid.): "Whoever accepts the hospitality of men of niggardly spirit
transgresses a prohibition, as it is said (Prov. 23.6): 'Eat not the
bread of him that has a parsimonious eye and do not desire his dain-
ties . . . eat and drink, he says to you, but his heart is not with you.'"

Generally a niggardly person represses all feelings of compassion,
devoting all his efforts to increasing his own wealth. He will not lend
any article to anybody, and certainly not his money, unless he can
extract some gain from it. Often, because of his unbridled parsimony
and greed for gain, he utterly disregards any advantage that might
accrue to him by lending out his money, even where he would receive
interest (and transgress the prohibition against usury). Such a person
has been warned by Scripture (Prov. 22.28): "He that has a niggardly eye hastens after riches and does not know that want shall come
upon him."

Midrash Tanchuma (*Sidra Behar*) also identifies the person with
the "niggardly eye" who "hastens after riches" as a usurer who
rushes to become rich. His property is cursed, as Scripture continues: "He does not know that want shall come upon him." The
Sefer Hachinuch lays down that the trait of niggardliness sets up an
iron barrier between the person and the blessing that should come to
him. He also removes himself from Heavenly compassion, according
to *Chazal's* interpretation (Shabbath 151b) of the verse (Deut.
13.18): "'And He shall give you mercy and have compassion on
you and multiply you.' He who is merciful to others, mercy is shown
to him by Heaven; while he who is not merciful to others, mercy is
not shown to him by Heaven." *Chazal* have also declared (Arachin
16a): "For seven things the plague of leprosy is incurred and one of
them is niggardliness (the person begrudging others will not allow
his neighbors to borrow and use his utensils [Rashi]), as it is written

(Lev. 14.35): 'Then *he who owns* the house shall come out and tell the priest saying: There seems to me to be as it were a plague in the house.' And it was taught in the Academy of R. Yishmael: (He was punished because) the house was reserved for his own use exclusively (i.e. he would not allow others to receive any benefit from it [Rashi]). Now, as is known, this house will have to be demolished, as Scripture states: 'And he shall break down the house, and its stones and its timber and all the mortar of the house.' In our days, however, even though the Holy One, blessed be He, does not want plagues to infect buildings, nevertheless a curse is brought down on the person's possessions and they are destroyed, as in the Midrash I have cited above. This is measure for measure. Since he is parsimonious, refuses to have pity or compassion on his neighbor and denies him the use of his property, then the force of pure justice, unmitigated by any *chesed*, shall hold sway over his property. Inevitably, then, his home will be destroyed on that account since, as we know, the world cannot endure if the force of pure justice by itself holds sway. In the *Pesikta* we find: "It happened that a person owned considerable possessions. He had a bad character and never gave charity. One day he became insane. He took a brand and set fire to his properties. He seized his silver and gold and cast them into the sea. He snatched an axe and smashed all his barrels of liquor. What caused all this to happen? Since this miser did not honor God while he possessed his wealth, these consequences followed upon his unwillingness to dispense charity and kindness to others."

The *Yalkut* (*Re'eh*), which we have quoted previously, declares: "Beware lest you withhold compassion, for anyone who withholds compassion identifies himself with idolatry and casts off the yoke of the Kingdom of Heaven, as it is said, '*Beli-ya'al*' "(i.e. without, *bli*; a yoke, *'ol*). The passage conveys that the parsimonious person relies on his money only, not on *Hashem* and His Torah. Against this, a warning is intimated in the verse (Exod. 21.23): "Gods of silver and gods of gold you shall not make for yourselves."

For a person not to have compassion and pity for the poverty and distress of another is in itself a culpable offence. See what is explicitly related (2 Sam. Chap. 12) concerning Nathan the prophet, who came to King David and told him of the poor man who owned only a single lamb. Because of his abject poverty, he raised it, fed it from his own loaf, let it drink from his own cup. Then came a wealthy man and stole it from him and slaughtered it. In passing sentence on the robber, David cried out: "As God lives, the man that has done this deserves to die . . . because he had no pity." A further examination of this passage reveals that the main reason for the offender being sentenced to death was his lack of pity for the poor (he had already been fined four sheep for the robbery and slaughter). (Note: How deeply and constantly should we meditate on this passage. To withhold pity is a very frequent occurrence, because of our many sins, and is involved in thousands of actions and with far-reaching consequences.)

Occasionally, it happens that the miser not only represses his own feelings of pity and compassion, but also influences his associates to withhold help from the less fortunate. He does not want to appear the wicked one. So he reviles any one who does differently. He becomes the embodiment of the description (Avoth 5.13): "He who will not give and does not wish others to give is a wicked man."

Sometimes his niggardly nature gains such control over him that he even begrudges himself the benefit of his possessions. Concerning him, Scripture has this to say (Eccl. 6.1 ff.): "There is a sore evil. . .a man to whom God gives riches, wealth and honor. . .yet God does not give him the power to eat thereof . . ." A force from the nether regions has gained control over him, as is shown by the Zohar (Beshallach 65 a/b): "R. Abba discoursed on the verse (Eccl. 5.13): 'There is a sore evil which I have seen under the sun, namely riches kept for the owners thereof to their own hurt.' 'There is a sore evil' — Are there then two kinds of evil, one that is sore and another that is not sore? Yes, indeed. There is a particular sore evil, for we have a tradition that from the Side of the Left emanate many emissaries of punishment who go down to the hollow of the great sea and then emerge in a body and, cleaving the air, advance on the sons of man. Each one of them is called 'evil' and it is to this that the words (Ps. 90.10) 'There shall no evil befall you' refer. When a certain one of these evils befalls a man, it makes him miserly with his money, so that when a collector of charity or a poor man comes to him, it strikes his hand saying: Do not impoverish yourself. It will not even let him buy favor for himself. In fact, from the moment that the 'evil' comes up on the man, he is 'sore' like a sick man who can neither eat nor drink. King Solomon proclaimed this in his wisdom (Eccl. 6.1-2): 'There is a sore evil which I have seen under the sun ... A man to whom God has given riches, wealth and honor, so that he lacks nothing for himself of all that he desires, yet God gives him no power to eat thereof but a stranger eats it' ... Because he entrusted himself to that evil and clings to it, God gave him no power over that evil to break from under it and he clings to it. (Because, when at first this evil enticed him not to do good to his fellow, he accepted the idea and followed this way—therefore God does not give him the power over this trait.) All his ways are like a sick man who does not eat or drink and keeps away from his money and watches it until he leaves this world and another man comes and takes possession of it and becomes its master. And King Solomon cries out and says: 'There is a sore evil ... riches kept for the owners thereof to his hurt ...' Who is the owner? The other that inherited it. Why did he deserve to become the owner of that wealth? Because this one believed that evil, wanted it and clung to it. Therefore the other who did not cling to that evil was worthy to become the owner of that wealth. That is what is conveyed by 'for his hurt.' "

Therefore a man should keep away from miserliness. He should always train himself to be goodhearted and to help others. He should not impair his sense of pity. Then others will have compassion on him too, as it is written (Ps. 125.4): "Do good O God unto the good . . ." He should always realize that the money given to him by God, may He be blessed, was not given to him for his own use alone, but to dispense charity and to engage in *gemiluth chesed*, as we shall prove from Biblical verses and Rabbinic literature. Then it will be well with him in this world and the next.

11

THE EXCUSE OF INDOLENCE REFUTED:
THE ENERGETIC PURSUIT OF THE SERVICE OF GOD

INDOLENCE. Some people are prevented from engaging in *Gemiluth Chesed* not by their unwillingness to let their money (the $50 or $100) lie idle and not earn income, but because they are too lazy to bother with having to give the loan and then having to go after the debtor to collect their money. Upon examination, we find that indolence is indeed the most frequent cause of preventing man from serving God. Through laziness, man remains devoid of Torah, of mitzvoth, of *teshuvah*; since it is the nature of the indolent always to postpone all things till tomorrow and the day after. King Solomon has described such a person (Prov. 24.3 ff.): "I went by the field of the slothful . . . and lo, it was all grown over with thistles . . . and the stone wall thereof was broken down."

Chazal have declared that four matters require extra exertion. They are: Torah study, good deeds, prayer, good manners. One must expend especially more effort than normal to habituate himself to good deeds. If he allows himself, God forbid, to weaken, then, as *Chazal* have stated in the name of Shmuel (Berachoth 63a), he will have no strength to stand up in the day of trouble (i.e. when any judgment threatens him), as it is said (Ps. 24.10): "If you are faint in the day of adversity, your strength will be small." Scripture has also declared (Prov. 2.4): "If you seek her as silver, and search for her as hidden treasure, then shall you understand the fear of *Hashem* and find the knowledge of God."

One should therefore conduct himself in affairs of Torah and mitzvoth with the same diligence as he does in his own business. Suppose, for instance, he owned a store. He would not hesitate to stand
behind the counter in cold weather. He would weigh out a quantity
for one customer, then for a second, for a third and so on ... even
though his profit on each sale was rather small. He would sit expec-
tantly, waiting for customers to come, and when they appeared, he
would be so overjoyed that he would not feel the cold. The reason for
his conduct is that he considers that his life depends on it, even
though this life is only momentary. How much more should one urge
himself on to action in the affairs of Torah and mitzvoth, to pursue
after them, and to take hold of them, as Scripture expresses it (Hos.
6.3): "And let us know, eagerly strive to know God." The effort
should not be a burden to him. So if it would happen that the borrower did not repay his debt, and had to be reminded over and over
again, nevertheless the lender should not on that account weaken his
commitment to this mitzvah of *gemiluth chesed*, just as a shopkeeper
would never abandon his store just because he has to expend effort
in collecting outstanding debts.

Obviously, practically no business is conducted without credit accounts. No business is operated without effort. Nor is there any
business which does not, upon occasion, incur a loss. What will you
argue?—that the storekeeper makes an overall profit from his
business? He earns a living in this world? But you, my friend, earn
eternal life—you assure that your soul will be bound in the bond of
eternity with *Hashem*, your God. As for that storekeeper, if he has to
exert a greater effort in collecting his debts, his profit is not proportionately increased even by one iota. In our case, however, the
greater the effort in performing the Divine mitzvah, the greater the
mitzvah itself becomes, as we find (Avoth 5.23): "According to the
labor is the reward."

Collecting the money owed to him will allow the giver to lend it
out again, as the Torah has intimated by (Exod. 22.25): "If you take

a pledge . . ." following immediately after "If you lend money to my people . . .", the implication being, according to the *Mechilta* (Ibid.) that one should first give the loan and then take a pledge. (The pledge here referred to can only be exacted with the permission of the Beth Din. As is pointed out in the *Gemara* [Bava Metzia 113b], to take a pledge without the authorization of the Beth Din is to transgress the prohibition [Deut. 24.10]: "You shall not go into his house to fetch the pledge." Even to seize a pledge from the debtor in the street is forbidden, as is laid down in *Choshen Mishpat*, Chap. 97 [q.v.].) This refutes the illusory belief that it were better for the lender to allow the money not to be repaid, since then he would not be obliged to bother lending it out again. The Torah teaches us proper conduct. It is better to keep claiming the money till it is recovered, and then to lend it out once more.

In this chapter I have described some of the types of indolence that the *yetzer harah* induces in people. Indeed there are many more such instances of human laziness leading to negligence in this mitzvah. One must, instead, follow the example set in the eager pursuit of worldly gain. In this way must we preoccupy ourselves with eternal values. Once man has accustomed himself to this behavior, the Biblical promise will be fulfilled for him (Prov. 2.5): "Then you shall understand the fear of *Hashem*, and find the knowledge of God."

12

THAT MAN SHOULD STRIVE TO FULFILL
THIS MITZVAH EVERY DAY

We have explained the great significance of the virtue of *chesed* in the previous chapters. It is effective in prolonging a person's life, in atoning for his sins. It protects him from all manner of plagues. Man thereby comes to shelter under the "shadow" of God Himself, may He be blessed, and not under the shadow of cherubim. He enjoys the fruit of his actions in this world, while the stock remains for him in the world to come. He succeeds in raising wealthy and wise sons . . . He is worthy of vindication in the final judgment and he obtains other exalted benefits as well. How intensely should one strive to embody this holy trait in himself and to love it intensely, as Scripture lays down (Micah 6.1): "What does God want of you but to do justice, to love *chesed*," for this mitzvah stands by man till the end of all generations, as we have explained in Chapter 4.

One should be especially careful not to neglect practising *chesed* even for a single day of his life, in the same way that one takes care to set fixed times for daily Torah study. I have found in *Sefer Hakedushah* of R. Chaim Vital that, every day, one should bemoan: "Woe is me! Another day has passed by without Torah and *gemiluth chesed*." The tenor of the statement is that the power of holiness in the world is brought to the full by the three chief preoccupations: Torah study, the Temple service, and *gemiluth chesed*. The second activity, the Temple service, has been denied to us, as a result of the multitude of our sins, since the day of the destruction.

Since only two activities now remain, we must reinforce them all the more. Then our iniquities will be forgiven, as the Biblical verse expresses it (Prov. 16.6): "By *chesed* and truth iniquity is expiated." *Chazal* (Berachoth 5b) explain *chesed* here to be the same as the *chesed* referred to in (Ibid. 21.21): "He that pursues after charity and lovingkindness (*chesed*) finds life, prosperity and honor," while "truth" refers to Torah, as is evident from the verse (Prov. 23.23): "Buy the truth and sell it not . . ."

"R. Yochanan b. Zakkai and R. Yehoshua b. Chananya stood near the Temple Mount. R. Yehoshua complained: Woe to us! The place where our iniquities were expiated is desolate. R. Yochanan b. Zakkai replied: My son, be not grieved. We possess an equally effective means of atonement. This is *gemiluth chesed*, as it is written (Hos. 6.6): 'For I desire *chesed* and not sacrifice.' " Now *chesed* secures atonement as effectively as sacrifices. And the altar was never without sacrifices on any single day; therefore, since everyone sins every day, he is obliged to practice this virtue every day. We constantly deplore the fact that we have neither Temple nor sacrifices at present. Because of the multitude of our sins, our iniquities proliferate every day. Hence man stands in ever greater compelling need of this holy trait to secure forgiveness of his sins. Even when the Temple stood, the people of those days needed to strive after these holy virtues of goodness and kindness all the days of their lives, as the Torah explicitly states (Deut. 11.22): "For if you diligently keep all these commandments . . . to love *Hashem* your God, to walk in all His ways all the days. . ." We have also explained according to the *Sifrei* that "walking in all His ways" refers to the "acquiring of the characteristics of *Hashem*, may He be blessed, which are the ways of goodness and kindness."

The reason for all this is, as the *Zohar* informs us, that man's days on this world have a permanence. From each day a spiritual creation comes into existence. And in the future, when the time arrives for man to leave the world, all his days appear before the Lord of all things to give evidence concerning him. Hence man must take care to keep all his days completely holy. From the daily study of Torah, he attains to the love of God, as we have deduced from the *Sifrei* (Deut. 6.6) on the verse: "And you shall love *Hashem*, your God," and similarly through the performance of mitzvoth, as *Chazal* have declared (Megillah 27a): "Great is study since it leads to action." One should also strive to cling to the Divine attributes, which are goodness and kindness alone. Then one will be worthy to have God cause the light of His countenance to shine upon him, as Scripture expresses it (Isa. 58.10): "And if you draw out your soul to the hungry, and satisfy the afflicted soul, then shall your light rise in darkness . . . and satisfy your soul in drought." This is why *Chazal* have stated so many times, "Whoever *occupies* himself with Torah study and *gemiluth chesed*." They did not word it: "Whoever has studied Torah and has performed acts of kindness." They wanted to show that one must constantly be prepared and ready for these activities. So, too, *Chazal* have stated (Bava Bathra 10a): "Whoever is habituated to give charity . . .", and they adduced their proof from the verse (Prov. 21.21) "Whoever pursues righteousness . . .", i.e. he pursues this holy virtue constantly.

We have dwelt at length on this subject to remove the erroneous idea entrenched in certain minds, viz. that after a person has once practised *gemiluth chesed* towards another, he has discharged his obligation for several weeks to come, even though he still is capable of doing good to others. On the contrary, every day of his life, whenever the need presents itself to him, he is obliged to fulfill the mitzvah, as long as he has the means, even if he is called upon several times on a single day. So we have recorded in our "Laws Governing Loans" (Chap. 1, Par. 1; cf. Ibid).

Now if a person were to scrutinize the days of his life that have already passed, in this light, he would find most of them devoid of this holy trait, and some of them even empty of Torah and the fear of God. He should therefore strive to sanctify the remaining days of his life, not to allow another day to pass without Torah study and *chesed*. One should not wonder how it would be possible to perform acts of *chesed* on the Sabbath, for this virtue includes a variety of activities beside free loans, as we have explained in our introduction.

We can perceive the greatness of these two activities: Torah study and *chesed*. God has shown us through the very beginning of the Hebrew alphabet that they are of paramount importance in rendering service to Him. So *Chazal* have discovered (Shabbath 104a ff.): "Children have come to the Beth Hamidrash and said things the like of which was not said even in the days of Joshua the son of Nun. *Alef Beth* means learn wisdom (*Alef binah*). *Gimmel Daled*, show kindness to the poor (*Gemol dalim*) (i.e. he should act benevolently towards the poor. Even though acts of *chesed* are to be extended to the rich as well [Sukkah 49], nevertheless the mitzvah is greater when the poor are helped, as the *Gemara* [Bava Metzia 71a] puts it: "A rich and a poor man—the poor comes first".) Why is the foot of the *Gimmel* stretched towards the *Daled*?—because it is fitting for the kind to run after the poor. And why is the roof of the *Daled* stretched to the *Gimmel*?—because the poor must make himself available to the benefactor. And why is the face of the *Daled* turned away from the *Gimmel*?—because he must give him in secret, lest he be ashamed of him. *Hei Vav* that is the Name of the Holy One, blessed be He." The idea, it seems to me, can be elucidated by reference to the statement of *Chazal* (Bava Bethra 75b): "The righteous are destined to be called by the Name of God, as it is said (Isa. 43.7): 'Every one that is called by My Name, whom I have created for My glory...'" Now the meaning of *Alef Binah Gemol Dalim* is that by Torah study and *gemiluth chesed*, *Hei Vav* (the Name of God) will be called on you in the time to come. (For God Himself studies the Torah every day, as we find in the *Gemara* [Avodah Zarah 4b], and God also feeds and sustains all the inhabitants of the world in His kindness and goodness, as we find in Scripture [Ps. 136.25]: "Who gives food to all flesh, for His *chesed* endures forever".) In *Tanna debei Eliyahu*

(Chap. 13), we find that the Holy One, blessed be He says to man: "My son, why have you not learned from your Father in Heaven? Sitting on His throne, He studies Scripture and Talmud for a third of the day; He pronounces judgment for the next third; and He dispenses charity and feeds and sustains all the inhabitants and all the work of His hands in the world, during the last third. If a man declares before God that he has studied Torah ever since he was thir teen years old, God will ask him: 'What have you accomplished by your learning?' (i.e. he will have to state the Scripture and Talmud he has studied, as *Tanna debei Eliyahu* declares in another context) and what good conduct have you engaged in? Have you not occupied yourself with idle conversation and unworthy and unbecoming remarks? As the prophet has stated (Amos 4.13): 'For lo, He Who forms the mountains and creates the wind, and declares unto man what is his conversation' " (Cf. ibid.).

See how great is the reward for Torah and *chesed*! The Gemara (Ibid.) expounds the significance of all the letters of the alphabet in sequence, and continues with *Zayin Cheth Teth Yod Kaf Lamed*: "If you do thus, the Holy One blessed be He will sustain (*Zan*) you, and be gracious (*Chen*) unto you, show goodness (*me-Tiv*) to you, give you a heritage (*Yerushah*) (this is what is stated in the Gemara [Bava Kamma 17a]: "Whoever is occupied with Torah study and *gemiluth chesed* is worthy of inheriting the understanding of Issachar), and bind a crown (*Keter*) on you in the world to come.

The meaning of this passage is that a man should not fear that through extending charity and making loans, his capital and his food will be diminished, or that through occupying himself with Torah he has to worry where his bread will come from. The passage answers the argument by saying, "The Holy One Blessed be He will feed you." Contrary to what you think, your performance of these acts will bring increase to your possessions. (As *Chazal* have declared (*Sifrei* Deut. 14.22): "Give a tithe ['*aser*], so that you will become wealthy [*titasher*]"— and the same applies to *chesed,* as we have written above, in Chapter 6.) Similarly, in regard to Torah, when a person studies constantly, he will not consequently, God forbid, suffer financial loss. *Chazal* have indicated that for this purpose God commanded the placing of the jar of manna 'before *Hashem'* (Exod. 16.33 ff.) as a lesson to the generations to come.

The prophet Jeremiah thereby demonstrated to the people of Israel that, without natural causes, the Holy One blessed be He would be able to provide the sustenance of the entire population as in the days of old (See Rashi Ibid.). And the *Gemara* (Shabbath 104b) quoted above expressed it precisely by saying: "The Holy One blessed be He sustains you," meaning that your food will come to you by supernatural means. "He will put a crown upon you, just as a father himself crowns his beloved son." Here is what Scripture says (1 Sam. 2.30): "For them that honor Me I will honor" (i.e. God Himself will bestow the honor directly—not through any agent). "And they that despise Me *shall be* lightly esteemed" (indirectly; God will not directly humiliate them but will hide His Presence from them and, in the natural course of events, they will be put to shame). For the measure of good exceeds the measure of punishment.

13

THE WORTHINESS OF SETTING ASIDE PART
OF ONE'S MONEY FOR LOANS

The last chapter has revealed many true insights into the greatness of the virtue of *chesed* and the duty to engage in it whenever the opportunity presents itself. We have also clearly demonstrated the fallacies in the *yetzer harah's* arguments against these worthy acts. How worthy would it be, therefore, for a person whom God has blessed with adequate means, to set aside a sum of money in his home (each person according to what he can afford) for a permanent *Gemiluth Chesed* Fund. This practice would produce many benefits. Firstly, the *yetzer harah,* as everyone knows, invents all kinds of excuses and rationalizations to dissuade one from performing this mitzvah, as we have explained in previous chapters. It is extremely difficult for a man to resist its persuasion at all times. And even if he should be willing to give, the members of his household might not allow him. They will cast suspicion on any person who approaches him. This would not happen if the money were already set aside. Then the person would find no difficulty in complying with all the requirements of the law.

I know that the reader will think to himself: "Why should I set a sum aside like the Free Loan Societies in each city, and then hand out small loans? It is better for me to lend a large, single sum which I can afford, as a single loan, to a respectable person, for after all *gemiluth chesed* is a mitzvah whether the loan is made to the poor or the rich." This is a fallacy. Firstly, it is a greater mitzvah to lend to the poor. *Chazal* have explained the verse (Exod. 22.24): "When you lend money to any of My people, to the poor with you . . ." to imply that if there are rich and poor, the poor take precedence (Bava Metzia 71a). Now where a person could not allocate more than a modest sum out of his capital, then if he were to loan it to the rich, there would remain nothing for him to loan to the poor. Scripture has taught that (Prov. 2.5): "If you seek her as silver . . . then shall you understand the fear of God." In business, if one engages in a number of small transactions involving a certain amount, the total profit will be larger than if the whole amount would be used in a single transaction. So too in our context, when the person gives a number of loans, each for a small amount as is customary, he can perform hundreds of positive mitzvoth of the Torah in the course of one year. This would not be so if he lent a single large sum to one individual. In the same period, he might only perform a few mitzvoth. Similarly, the *Tanna* (Pirkei Avoth 3.15) has laid down that "the world is judged by grace, yet all is in accord with the majority of deeds" (i.e. the world is judged according to which number of deeds is the larger, if the good, then the judged shall emerge victorious from their trial). The Rambam (ad loc.) has noted that the Mishnah does not read "the greatness of the deed" (but "the majority"), since the performance of many good deeds is preferable, even though each act by itself is of less significance, than the performance of one single, great deed. So in our case, suppose one man had given out many small amounts as charity to each of a large number of people. The total added up to, say $100. Another person gave a lump sum of $100 to a needy member of a respectable family. The second lender has certainly fulfilled the dictates of the law, since this is the amount appropriate to the case. Nevertheless the merit earned by the first lender by far exceeds his. By performing many good deeds commanded by God, his soul becomes exalted because he has acquired merit on its behalf. He thereby attains holiness, as it is said (Num. 15.40): "So that you may remember and do all my commandments and be holy unto your God." Furthermore, the first lender has, by his many deeds, habituated himself to do good, and has ingrained this trait in his soul much more than has the second lender, who overcame his evil tendencies only once. Hence, in the Heavenly accounts of the mitzvoth, the latter's action only counts as one. So, too, in granting loans, the person who sets aside a sum of money so as to give a small amount to each person requesting a loan, will, in the course of time, accumulate many hundreds of mitzvoth. This will not be so if he lends a large, single sum to a more respectable person.

Another advantage is that once the money has been set aside, the other members of his family can also participate in the mitzvah, for instance, when he is away on business or when he is asleep. Other people, too, will learn to emulate his act, and he will be acceptable to God, since he has set the example. This is the meaning of the statement (Avoth 4.13): "R. Shimon said: There are three crowns: the crown of learning, the crown of priesthood, and the crown of royalty; but the crown of a good name exceeds them all." The good name a person acquires by his good deeds will stimulate others to imitate him and the Name of Heaven will thereby be sanctified. It seems to me that this is what *Chazal* (Shabbath 153a) meant: "Which man has earned the world to come?—(Isa. 20.21): 'And your ear shall hear a word behind you saying, this is the way; walk in it.'"

On the verse (Prov. 22.1): "It is better to choose a good name than riches," *Midrash Tehillim* (ad loc.) gives this comment: "Come and see how weighty is a good name. Even if a man owns thousands of golden dinars, but does not have a good name, he has acquired nothing." The reason: His failure to acquire a good name must have resulted from his failure to use his money for charitable and free loan purposes. Of what use, then, was all his property?—only to bring him to account for not having carried out the instructions of the party who deposited the money with him. Indeed, the amount of money owned by a person in excess of his needs is a trust fund deposited by the Master of the Universe, Who appointed him to administer it, to take pity on the unfortunate and to extend favors to the needy. On the verse (Exod. 22.24) "When you lend money to My people, the poor man that is with you," R. Mosheh Alshech has commented: "This is comparable to a person who has deeded all his money to one of his sons. [The law presumes that] he only intended to appoint this son a trustee, since it is reasonable to assume that he would not cut off the rest without anything. Hence the share of each of the other sons is held to be a trust fund kept with him. So in our case: God made one person rich. Is it possible to assume that he has left the rest in penury? Are they not his sons as well? God, then, appointed the rich person a trustee to support the poor, and their share with him exceeds his own portion." This is what the verse (Ibid), "the poor that is *with you*," conveys: Whatever the poor really needs belongs to him. It is deposited with you on his behalf, therefore you must not withhold it from him.

Even if, through his constant preoccupation with this *mitzvah*, a person might occasionally incur a loss of money, he should not suffer grief, since obviously no business in the world, whether it be a store or other enterprise, large or small, can entirely avoid bad debts and other such losses. Very few undertakings are fully guaranteed against any loss whatever. Nevertheless a very large section of the world engages in business, day and night, since it is not necessary to consider one solitary, occasional transaction, but rather the overall operation of the business, to determine whether it is profitable or not.

It is recommended that each person decide to allocate a sum of a few dollars towards this activity each year (the rich to set aside proportionately larger amounts). In this way, even if the mitzvah does cause an occasional loss to occur, he will not be grieved, since he had already agreed to part with this money—just as he has no regrets for having spent money on his *tefillin*.

The assertion of *Chazal* (Bava Bathra 10a) is also well known: "In the same way as a man's earnings are determined for him from Rosh

Hashanah so are his losses determined for him from Rosh Hashanah. If he finds merit in the eyes of Heaven, then (Isa. 58.7): 'deal out your bread to the poor,' but if not He 'will bring the wailing poor into his house' (Rashi [Bava Bathra 9a] explains that the "wailing poor" refer to Roman tax collectors). A case in point is that of the nephews of R. Yochanan b. Zakkai. He saw in a dream that they were to lose 700 dinars in that year. He accordingly forced them to give him money for charity until only 17 [of the 700] dinars were left. On the eve of Yom Kippur the government arrested them. R. Yochanan b. Zakkai said to them: Do not fear. You had to give 17 dinars and these they have taken away. They said to him: How did you know that this was going to happen? He replied: I saw it in a dream. Then why did you not tell us? they asked. Because, he said, I wanted you to perform the mitzvah for its own sake."

We shall now proceed to explain the term, "his losses," mentioned in this passage. Is man compelled to incur losses? Let God bestow less benefits and no losses? The meaning is: There is, after all, no completely righteous person in the world. Everyone is forced to cleanse himself of his sins and to suffer pain in the process. However, God commutes this bodily suffering to a loss of property. As the *Tanna debei Eliyahu* expresses it: "Everyone is sold and redeemed every day, as it is said (Ps. 31.6): 'Into Your hand I recommend my spirit; You have redeemed me, O God of truth.' " This quotation implies that the soul ascends to heaven each day to sign the register of its deeds. Its iniquities make it liable to be handed over to harmful powers. ("Sold" is used here in the sense of "being handed over" as in the verse [Judges 4.9]: "For God will sell [hand over] Sisera into the hand of a woman.") God in His infinite mercies, however, rescues the soul from extreme punishment and commutes the sentence to some severe grief or loss of property. The person who is worthy incurs the loss of property in the performance of a mitzvah, such as charity or *gemiluth chesed*. Such a loss is a gain to him, for several reasons. Firstly, he has acquired a mitzvah of the Torah; he has exchanged his dross for precious metals. Secondly, a mitzvah which costs money is more valuable than one which does not, as the *Zohar* (*Sidrah Terumah*) explains. Thirdly his financial loss will only be temporary. The Holy One blessed be He will surely repay double his outlay, as Scripture promises (Deut. 15.10): "You shall surely give him and your heart shall not be grieved when you give him; because for this thing *Hashem* your God will bless you in all your work."

We have dwelt at length on all these details to make everyone realize what lies in store for him. Ultimately, it is inevitable that man suffer some loss, some reduction of his property, as punishment for his sins. He thereby escapes being condemned to *Gehennom*, or some other grievous punishment. Why should he then close his fist against giving charity or granting loans? He would otherwise be forced to bring the "wailing poor" into his house, or else to call a physician for someone in his family, as *Chazal* have asserted (Num. Rabba 11.13): "The house that is closed to the poor is open to the physician." Is it not better to be forewarned—to open one's house to the poor and to set aside sums of money for loans? The wise will then reap all the benefits.

14

MORE ON THE SUBJECT OF CHESED

We shall return to the subject of *gemiluth chesed*, acts of benevolence. We know that we have not yet succeeded in removing all obstacles from our path. The *yetzer harah* can appear in another guise and argue: "Why should you be more righteous and saintly than everyone else? Those people are richer than you are, and they are not at all concerned with charitable and benevolent endeavor! Each one of them accumulates wealth which he will bequeath to his children. Be like them. You will still be able, upon occasion, to do good to others." Now let me answer you.

Suppose two people were to approach you and offer you an opportunity to invest in real estate. Both assured you that the value of the property would appreciate considerably in the course of time. Both enjoyed the widest reputation as bona-fide dealers, and as most competent experts in the real estate business. You, yourself, trust implicitly that not a single word they have told you will prove false. An independent dealer, the foremost of all the experts in the field, in the meantime, has also praised the offer very highly. Would you not rush post haste after this investment and close the deal, even though you would have to give a very considerable amount as a down payment? You would not consider that such an investment is better suited to other, larger investors—that success becomes them more than a small person like yourself. You would rejoice that God had granted you the opportunity to rise higher, to enjoy a reputation comparable to the rich.

My friend, as for pursuing after *chesed* with all your might, two of the world's most renowned persons, reliable, and expert in every type of wisdom—our forefather Abraham and King Solomon—have lavishly praised this occupation. They have disclosed that the highest pinnacle of success is achieved through such activity. Abraham, our forefather, of blessed memory, was first. He strove with all his might to do *chesed*. He benefitted men spiritually, by teaching them to know *Hashem*, and physically, by serving them food and drink, by bringing them into his home and by treating them with respect and deference. He even planted a tree for their comfort. All these acts emanated from the goodness and kindness in his character. He also enjoined his children to continue along the same lines. He assured them of success in their efforts. And in this way, all the blessings with which God had blessed him would be passed on to them.

As for King Solomon, of blessed memory, he asserted that whoever pursued charity and *chesed* would find life, righteousness and honor. (If only sporadic rather than constant preoccupation with this mitzvah is required, then the word "pursue" would be inappropriate.) Furthermore, the Great Guide, the Supreme Head of all, the Holy One, blessed be He, has given His approval to this activity. He said (Gen. 18.17): "Shall I hide from Abraham that which I am doing; seeing that Abraham shall surely become a great and mighty nation, and all the nations of the earth shall be blessed in him? For I have known him to the end that he will command his children and his household after him, that they may keep the way of God, doing charity and justice, so that God may bring upon Abraham in the end that which he has spoken of to him." From this verse the *Gemara* (Yevamoth 79a) deduces that the same results will be achieved by the person engaging in *gemiluth chesed*, since both charity and *chesed* have this in common, the doing of good to others. What more need we say on the subject?

Scripture has also intimated that the person engaging in this endeavor bequeaths a good inheritance to his children after him, which lasts to the end of all generations, as we find (Ps. 103.17): "But the benevolence of God is from everlasting to everlasting towards them that fear Him." This verse refers to the person occupied with *chesed*, as the *Yerushalmi* (Peah 1.1) explains. It is not like the purchase of real estate which can pass out of one's own hands even during his lifetime, and certainly after his death.

Come and take heed of what is recounted in *Massechet Kallah* (Chap. 9): "They said of R. Tarfon that he was extremely wealthy. Yet he did not give charity to the poor (as befitted his means). Once he met R. Akiva. The latter said to him: Rabbi, would you want me to purchase one or two cities for you? He said, Yes. Immediately, R. Tarfon handed him 4,000 golden dinars. R. Akiva took the money and distributed it among the poor. Some time later, R. Tarfon met him and asked: Where are the cities you bought with my money? He (R. Akiva) took him by the hand and led him to the Beth Hamidrash, brought out a Book of Psalms and opened it before them. They read in it until they reached the verse (Ps. 112.9): 'He scattered abroad, he gave to the poor; his *tzedakah* will endure for ever.' He (R. Akiva) said: This is the city which I bought for you. R. Tarfon stood up and kissed him. My master, my guide—he called him—My master in wisdom and my guide in good conduct. He (R. Tarfon) provided him with additional money to distribute [among the poor].

R. Akiva did not, God forbid, lie, even when he first said to R. Tarfon that he would purchase a city for him. What he had in mind was the angels and heavenly powers created by this holy, eternal *mitzvah*. (These heavenly beings are designated by the word "city" in the usage of the Midrash [*Tanchuma Vaethchanan* 2] in its comment on the verse (Prov. 21.22): "A wise man scales the city of the mighty . . .", where "city" refers to the angels and "wise man" to Moses.) The honor man receives there is eternal too. This is intimated by the verse (Ps. 112.9): "His *tzedakah* shall endure for ever, his horn shall be exalted in honor." R. Tarfon understood this and did not harbor resentment against R. Akiva, God forbid. His love for R. Akiva became stronger; he kissed him on the forehead for exchanging his ephemeral properties for eternal palaces. How fitting it is, then, for every person to build, while he is yet alive, an enduring home, *Heichal Hachesed*, a Palace of Benevolence for his soul.

Finally, it has been left us to deal with the evil inclination's attempt to persuade a person that he must preserve his possessions to bequeath a large inheritance to his children. But this too is a worthless argument. Should a person be cruel to himself because he loves his children? He is obliged to be kind to himself as well. Consider this case: Suppose someone was found guilty of treason. He was sentenced to be tortured—to be forced to stand on burning coals—or else to pay a heavy fine instead. Would anyone dare to think it better for him, because of his concern for his children, to suffer deathly pains rather than pay the fine? Is it not that (Job. 2.4): "Skin for skin, yes, all that a man has he will give for his life"? Even if the amount he was fined would equal his entire wealth, certainly if it was not more than half or a quarter of what he owned, he would gladly part with the money to escape the torture. He would not give a second thought to the fact that less money would now remain for his sons. If anyone advised him differently, he would consider that person a fool.

So now you should clearly understand what lies before you. You are well aware that the punishment of *Gehennom* is grievous and bitter. All who pass through it pour out tears like the fountains of the *Shittin* (giant pipes), as *Chazal* have pointed out. The other punishments meted out to man after death are also extremely severe. One is able to ransom one's soul, to avoid the ultimate suffering, by the constant stimulation of one's intelligence, during his lifetime, to devise ways and means of assisting the poor with charity and benevolence. Scripture (Ps. 41.2) expresses the idea in these words: "Happy is he who deals intelligently with the poor. God will deliver him in the day of evil." Evil here refers to *Gehennom* as in the verse (Prov. 16.4): "The wicked for the day of evil." How can a person fail to have pity on himself? How can he refuse to escape from *Gehennom* and all the other dire punishments? The verse (Isa. 58.7): "Hide not yourself from your own flesh," is explained by *Tanna debei Eliyahu* to mean that a person should not refrain from doing good to, and having pity on, himself. This agrees with the view we have expressed.

So, now, we have refuted all the possible arguments. If God has helped someone acquire great wealth and he has the time, then it is better for him to perform the mitzvah by himself rather than through an agent, as the *Gemara* (Kiddushin 41a) indicates. If he does not have the time, he should follow the example he himself has set in conducting his many business interests, i.e. having his employees carry out his directives.

To sum up: This occupation will affect a person forever. Why should he find it less important than his temporary, ephemeral interests?

If the person is unable to appoint an agent to conduct these activities for him, he should search the city for a trustworthy and God-fearing man who would be willing to occupy himself with this mitzvah. He should entrust the money he allocates for the performance of this mitzvah to this person's care.

All that we have discussed so far refers not only to a wealthy person. Even someone who is not well-to-do should set aside small amounts from his earnings, as we shall explain further on, and set up, in his own home, a permanent *Gemiluth Chesed* Fund to grant small loans as each case requires. Even if he lends a small sum to a poor man to prepare for Shabbath, he is fulfilling the positive mitzvah of the Torah, "When you lend money to My people . . ." It makes no difference whether one gives less or more as long as his intentions are pure. How good would it be if this custom were to become widespread among our people, the holy nation—if all were to engage in performing this mitzvah? The world would be filled with the virtue of *chesed*, and all trouble and tribulation would cease.

This, in my opinion, is what the passage in *Tanna debei Eliyahu* sought to convey: "When Israel was in Egypt, all gathered together ... and made a covenant together to act with *chesed* towards each other." That a covenant was made indicates that the entire population, whether of rich or modest means, did all in their power to be benevolent to one another. This is the *middah* of *chesed* which was one of the causes of the redemption of Israel, as I have cited above in the name of the *Pesikta*.

May the Allpresent in His mercy strengthen us to acquire this holy virtue, through which we shall become worthy of all the good of this world and the next.

15

CHESED SECURES ATONEMENT LIKE THE BRINGING OF SACRIFICES.
SEVERAL IMPORTANT POINTS CONCERNING *ISKA* LOANS

We have, with God's help, offered the good advice to everyone on how to increase the practice of *gemiluth chesed* in the world. It might, however, appear strange to the reader that we recommend the establishment of a *Gemiluth Chesed Fund* in the home of every person, rich or poor. To their surprise I answer: Suppose, my friend, that the Temple would have been re-established and the altar rebuilt in our days. How much effort would every person exert to visit Eretz Yisrael upon occasion or at least once during his lifetime, so as to bring his burnt- or sin-offering, whichever was needed, to secure atonement for himself. His journey, both ways, would entail considerable expense. Yet the cost would not seem excessive to him, or to anyone else. On the contrary, he would rejoice at having attained the merit of bringing an offering before *Hashem*, the King, for his sins. This indeed is man's life-purpose, to take care to rectify his iniquities in his own lifetime, that he should not appear repulsive to God, in whose eyes every evil is loathsome.

The same reasoning applies to the practice of *gemiluth chesed*. We are certain that everyone properly engaging in these activities will secure atonement for his sins, as effectively as if he had brought a sacrifice in times gone by, and even more so, as we find in *Avoth de R. Nathan* (Chap. 4.1): "Once R. Yochanan b. Zakkai was leaving

Jerusalem. R. Yehoshua was following behind him and saw the ruins of the Temple. R. Yehoshua said: Woe to us for this! The place where atonement was obtained for Israel's sins is in ruins. He replied: My son, let this not sadden you. We have another form of atonement which is equal to this. And what is it?—*gemiluth chesed*, as it is said (Hos. 6.6): 'For I desire *chesed* and not sacrifice.' "

Certainly, everyone whom God has favored with intelligence will take care not to neglect this activity. He will establish as large a permanent loan fund as he can afford within his home. In this way he will secure atonement for his sins, just as by means of the altar in ancient times.

I have dwelt at length on these matters so as to refute the arguments advanced by man's *yetzer harah*—views that are widespread in certain areas, because of our many sins, and which have caused people to do the opposite of everything desirable. As soon as a person has saved a few dollars, the *yetzer harah* persuades him not to lend the money to anyone, even the most reliable person. Instead, the owner takes it to a money-lender to earn an income from it. Great harm results from this practice, because of our many sins. The depositors are for the most part simple people who are unaware of the *Heter Iska*. When they approach a money-lender, they merely say: "Take the money and pay us interest." They take no precautions to obtain an *Iska* note in return, and only ask for a note recognized as valid by the State. This is utterly forbidden, as since they do not know what an *Iska* is nor do they obtain an *Iska* note. As is known, transgression of the prohibition against taking usury effects one's rights to resurrection, to *techiath hamethim*. Secondly, even where a valid *Heter Iska* is prepared, its use diminishes the amount of *chesed* in the world. And it has been recorded in the holy books that one of the purposes of the Torah in prohibiting usury was to increase the *chesed* in the world, so that God, may He be blessed, would also treat the world with *chesed*.

In former years this evil practice was not so widespread. Only the person who had accumulated large savings, and who used the income for his living expenses, would indulge in it. Certainly we cannot require a person to use up his entire capital in free loans. (In such a case, one should, however, be meticulously careful to fulfill the requirements of the law. See *Chochmath Adam.*) Today, however, the custom has gained such acceptance in certain areas that even those possessing a few dollars, whose profits will be insignificant, rush to the money-lender to put out their money at interest. And the virtue of *chesed* has almost lapsed into oblivion. For there is hardly any loan available except from money-lenders at interest.

My friends! My brothers! This is not what God chose or intended. True; the prohibition against usury is not transgressed. Yet, surely, if one is able to, he is obliged to lend his money charitably to a reliable person or to one offering him a pledge to insure him against loss, as was explained before in the "Laws Governing Loans, Chapter 1." One should trust in God, instead, and believe that by exercising the virtue of *chesed*, God will, in return, treat him with the attribute of *chesed* and bless him in all his undertakings.

Those conducting themselves to the contrary not only reduce the *chesed* in the world, but often, they are given a taste—in this world—of the fruits of their conduct and many of them lose money and fail even to recover their principal in the end. In them is the assertion of *Chazal* fulfilled (Bava Metzia 71): "The property of the usurers will eventually collapse." The *iska* lenders are similar to usurers in one respect: they abolish the virtue of *chesed*. And the *Gemara* (Kethuvoth 66b) quotes the proverb: "Whoever wishes to salt away his money shall reduce it (*chaser*); others read *chesed*, shall act benevolently with it." The maxim declares that by reducing his liquid capital, i.e. by using it for free loans and for charity, his money will remain with him. If he acts to the contrary, his money will be like "unsalted meat", it will decay of itself. (Here, because of our many sins, is one of the causes of poverty among Jews. Previously all loans were *gemiluth chasadim*. God governed us with *chesed*, accordingly. We were granted a year of business prosperity and blessing. This is not the case today because of our many sins.

Now we shall direct our attention to the lending of money for profit. First of all, the lender should ensure that the *Heter Iska* is legally valid. There should be no usury, as legally defined, in this transaction. Otherwise the lender will lose all his possessions, as the *Gemara* declares. Besides this he incurs a grievous punishment, the loss of his rights to resurrection. (*Chazal* relate that when Ezekiel revived the dead in the valley of Dura [Ezek. Chap. 37], all rose and stood erect, a great host, except for one individual who remained lying in the dust—he was a usurer.) Furthermore, his conduct is tantamount to signing with his own hand that he denies the God of Israel, as *Chazal* have asserted (Bava Metzia 71a. Cf. ibid). This is not the place to explain how ruinous is such behavior.

Because of our many sins, people have come to regard what is prohibited as permissible. They fail to realize that they are destroying their own lives. It is therefore the duty of everyone engaged in such moneylending to study the relevant *halachoth* in *Yoreh Deah* or *Chochmath Adam*. The person should also realize that he is not absolved from the positive commandment of "When you lend money to My people. . ." (as a free loan). He should make such loans according to his means. He should not decide that since money-lending is his business, his life takes precedence over his neighbor's. Now, we never intended to convey that one should lend out all his financial resources in free loans. We meant that one is obliged to perform this mitzvah of *gemiluth chesed* as far as his means allow. The shopkeeper, too, is bound to fulfill it, to the extent that he can afford, even though he could certainly use up all his money in purchasing inventory, and leave his household without a single dollar in cash. Nevertheless, if he can at all save a certain sum of money for making loans to others, he is obliged to do so, as I explained in the "Laws Governing Loans," Chapter 2.

Obviously a person constantly occupied in lending for profit will find it very difficult to overcome his drives and advance sums as *gemiluth chasadim*. For him, the best advice in this connection is to set aside a specific amount of money, in proportion to his means, for free loans, as we have suggested before. In this way he will encounter no resistance, since the money has already been allocated and he no longer regards it as his own. With the amount thus set aside, he should constantly practice *gemiluth chesed*, using the same energy as in his business loans. In this way the measure of *chesed* in the world will be increased. He will also make some amends for the damage caused by his numerous interest-bearing loans which diminish the quantity of *chesed* in the world, as was explained above. He should also devote himself energetically to performing the other types of *chesed* which are described further on in this *Sefer. Chazal* have declared, "The righteous gain acceptance through the very thing in which they have sinned."

16

THE OBLIGATION TO ESTABLISH
A GEMILUTH CHESED FUND IN EVERY CITY

Because of the extreme importance of the mitzvah of *gemiluth chesed*, we have devoted much attention to the need for every one to set aside a larger or smaller sum for a permanent free loan fund in his own home. Yet obviously not everyone can afford the money. Others again cannot afford the time the performance of the mitzvah entails. For those unable to establish such funds privately, the best advice is to band together to form a Free Loan Society to lend money to others in their hour of need. Indeed, it has been the custom throughout all the scattered Jewish communities to organize such a society in every city. To evaluate the greatness of the mitzvah performed by the members of a community in setting up such a fund is quite superfluous. Our introduction and many of the subsequent chapters have pointed out the grievous sin committed by anyone closing his fist against lending to others and the great reward earned by whoever fulfills this mitzvah. Naturally, then, no one with any intelligence will rest until he sees a Free Loan Society existing in his city to lend to the needy. In this way, his fellow citizens and he himself will avoid the possibility of committing a grave sin. For it could conceivably happen that a poor man would take his security pledge and approach several people for a loan. Each would offer another excuse for refusing. Then the poor man would return home crushed. He would cry out and remonstrate with God against his evil lot. And we know what Scripture has to say on this subject (Deut.

15.9): "Beware that there be not a base thought in your heart saying: 'The seventh year, the year of release is at hand'. . .and he cry unto God against you, and it be sin in you." The guilt will fall on everyone's neck since, on account of the frequency of such needs, all are duty bound to prevent such incidents.

I have taken it upon myself to demonstrate, for everyone's benefit, how much more effective is such a society than individuals sporadically performing the mitzvah. There are several reasons. First, as *Chazal* have said, it is better for many to be involved in the performance of a specific mitzvah, than for one person to perform the act by himself. Even though each individual contributes a very small amount to each loan, since many are participating, nevertheless the Holy One, blessed be He, apparently considers each participant as if he had personally advanced the entire sum, since without his contribution the poor man would not have obtained the required, full amount. Moreover, this mitzvah costs money; it is not free. Its reward, accordingly, is greater. So the *Zohar* (*Sidrah Terumah*), expounding the verse (Exod. 25.2): "That they take me an offering," reports: "This signifies that he who aspires towards piety and fellowship with the Holy One blessed be He must not be lax or remiss in his devotion, but must be ready and willing to bring sacrifices according to his strength, 'according as God blessed you' " (Deut. 16.10). True, it is written (Isa. 55.1) "Come and buy wine and milk without money and without cost," and this refers to work on behalf of the Holy One, blessed be He. But this only indicates that, whereas knowledge of the Holy One, blessed be He, and His Torah can be acquired without cost or fee, the doing of good works must be paid for with the full price; otherwise the doer of good works is not worthy to draw down to himself the spirit of holiness from above.

Moreover, this mitzvah can now be practised even while the person is preoccupied with his business or when he is asleep. In addition, there is the statement in the Midrash (*Koheleth Rabba*): "If a person longs and makes others long to perform mitzvoth, but has not accomplished a mitzvah that endures for generations, what benefit has he acquired?" Whoever has a share, however, in a communal mitzvah, like the one we have mentioned, or whoever has contributed to the support of Yeshivoth where Torah is studied, even if he has already earned the right to *Gan Eden*, his soul will receive additional delight and illumination, because of the mitzvoth constantly being performed with the money he contributed.

All who occupy themselves with this activity: the trustees, the collectors who canvass donors—all earn the very greatest reward. They are included among those designated as the pursuers of charity and *chesed* "who will find life, righteousness and honor." Trustees are regarded as charity treasurers. Concerning them, we find in *Midrash Tanchuma*, "What should someone do to remain alive if he was condemned to die by an act of God? — If he was accustomed to study chapter of the Mishnah, he should study two instead; one leaf of the Gemara—he should study two; and if he is not accustomed to study, he should become a charity treasurer and save his life, as it is said (Prov. 21.21): "He that pursues charity and *chesed* shall find life, righteousness and honor."

Fund raising involves causing others to perform a mitzvah. *Chazal's* statement (Sanhedrin 99b) in this connection is well known: "Rabbi Abahu said: Whoever causes (i.e. urges and encourages) his neighbor to perform a mitzvah is regarded as if he himself had performed it, as it is said, 'And your staff with which you smote the Nile.' Did Moses smite the Nile? Did not Aaron smite it?—This tells you that whoever causes another to perform a mitzvah is regarded by Scripture as if he had performed it himself." Consider therefore how much the collector achieves with every small amount he raises. In heaven the mitzvah is credited to him as well. In addition, he is one of the public benefactors who cause Israel to perform many hundreds of mitzvoth every year. And "Whoever causes the many to be righteous, no sin shall be brought about through him" (Avoth 5.18).

Chazal have also told us (Bava Bathra 9a): "R. Eliezer said: Greater is he who causes others to act than he who acts himself, as it is said (Isa. 32.17): 'And the work of charity shall lead to peace, and the effect of charity is quietness and confidence for ever.' " Now charity and *gemiluth chesed*, as is known, are similar and the raising of funds for *gemiluth chesed* is like soliciting for charity, since in both cases the money is not returned to the donor. In my opinion, the reason why the solicitor is greater than the donor is as follows. There are charity and *chesed* which the individual performs through his money, and there is *chesed* which the individual performs with his person, as we have explained in the introduction. Now the individual who raises money for charity has to approach several people. He has to speak to each one of them. So he fulfills the mitzvah of extending *chesed* with his person each time he approaches someone. His own mitzvah increases proportionately to the number of people he approaches; while each one of the donors only performs the single mitzvah of giving charity or a *gemiluth chesed* when he is approached.

Even if the solicitor is unable to contribute anything, and his only accomplishment is the encouragement of others to give, he too receives blessing from God for his deeds, as we find in the *Tosefta* (Peah Chap. 3): "Whoever pledged to give and gave, is granted reward for his pledge and for his deed. If he undertook to give but was unable to carry out his word, he will be rewarded for his word, as if the deed had been accomplished. He who did not pledge to give, but told others to give, will receive reward for this, as it is said: (Deut. 15.10) 'Because that for this word, *Hashem* your God will bless you.' " How much more will he be blessed if he also makes his own contribution, as we find (Avoth 5.13): "As to charity contributions, there are four dispositions:. . .he who wishes to give and wishes others to give is a *chasid*. . ." The Talmud adds (Bava Bathra ibid.): "Rava said to the inhabitants of Mechuza: Force each other to behave so that you may live in peace under the government." The meaning is that by each one compelling his neighbor to perform mitzvoth, they would be freed from other compulsory State services, for God will grant them peace under the government, as it is said (Isa. 32.17): "And the work of charity shall be peace." R. Yochanan b. Zakkai likewise forced his relatives to give charity. They had only to pay the balance to the heathen State, as we explained in Chapter 13.

Even if fund raising requires great effort, it should not be abandoned. "According to the pain is the reward" (Avoth 5.23). Even if certain people despise him, the fund raiser should take no notice. He should realize that his reward will be all the greater because he suffered humiliation for the sake of *Hashem*. A similar thought is expressed in *Yoreh Deah* (Chap. 257, Par. 7): "The charity treasurers should pay no heed if the poor revile them, since their merit is thereby increased." The same measure applies to our case. (I have found an allusion to the worthiness of causing others to perform good deeds in the Scriptural verse [Deut. 15.10]: "Therefore I command you *to say [to others]*: 'You shall surely open your hand' "—one should *say*, one should order and urge others to open their hands and contribute.) I have devoted considerable attention to this subject to demonstrate, for everyone's benefit, the great importance of arousing others to perform mitzvoth. All of this activity is included in the virtue of *chesed*. Yet people have the habit of avoiding the tasks of encouraging others to do mitzvoth even where the need is extremely urgent. As a result the mitzvah is not fulfilled. Such conduct is not at all commendable.

17

THE IMPORTANCE OF CHARITY

So far, we have explained the greatness of the virtue of *chesed*. Now we shall focus our attention on the subject of charity. *Chazal* have declared (Sukkah 49b): "*Gemiluth chesed* is greater than charity, since charity is performed with one's money, while *chesed* is exercised both with one's money and his person." ("With one's money" here includes lending cash, articles, or livestock. "*Gemiluth chesed*" both with one's money and his person—delivering a eulogy over the dead; acting as pall bearer; bringing joy to bride and groom; escorting one's neighbor on his journey—[Rashi].) Charity is given to the poor; *gemiluth chesed* is extended to poor and rich alike; charity is given to the living, *chesed* both to the living and the dead." Nevertheless charity is superior to *gemiluth chesed* in several respects. Charity is an outright gift, while a *gemiluth chesed* loan is advanced for a limited period after which the lender recovers his money. More effort is required to overcome one's *yetzer harah* in giving charity since one's net worth is thereby reduced (which is not so in *gemiluth chesed*), and according to the effort is the reward. As for the Talmudic statement (Shabbath 63a) that the one lending money to the poor is greater than the donor of an outright gift, this refers to a man who has become financially weakened through the loss of his possessions and now needs help to stand on his own feet. For him a loan is preferable to a gift. He is saved from being put to shame. On the other hand, the one who is reduced to penury and is already accustomed to accepting charity is better served by an out-

right gift than by a loan. Understood in this way, the exposition of
the verse (Deut. 30.15): "See I have set before you this day, life and
good, and death and evil", in *Pirkei De R. Eliezer* (Chap. 15),
becomes clear: "The Holy One blessed be He said: Behold these two
ways I have given Israel, one is good, the other evil. The one which is
good is of life; and the one which is of evil is of death. The good way
has two byways: one of charity, the other of *chesed.* Elijah, be he
remembered for good, is placed exactly between these two ways.
When a man comes to enter [one of them], Elijah cries aloud concerning him, saying: 'Open you gates that the righteous nation which
keeps truth may enter in' (Isa. 26.2). And there comes Samuel the
prophet and he places himself between these two byways. He says:
On which of these two byways shall I go? If I go the way of charity,
then the path of *chesed* is better than the former; if I go the way of
chesed, the way of charity is better. But I call on heaven and earth to
be my witness that I will not give up either of them. I shall appropriate both of them for myself. The Holy One blessed be He says:
Samuel, you stood between the two good byways. By your life, I
shall grant you three good gifts. This is to teach you that whoever
desires and performs deeds of charity and *chesed* inherits three good
gifts, and they are 'life, righteousness and honor,' as it is said: 'He
who pursues charity and *chesed* will find life, righteousness and
honor.' " Therefore man should most energetically pursue charity.

We could never find enough space to copy down all the Rabbinic
references to charity; I shall only repeat a few of them. In *Tanna
debei Eliyahu Zuta* (Chap. 1) they stated in the name of the
Academy of Eliyahu: "Great is the power of charity since, from the
day of the creation until now, the world has been held up by charity.
Everyone who gives much is praiseworthy and rescues himself from
the punishment of *Gehennom,* as it is said (Eccl. 11.10): 'Therefore
remove vexation from your heart and put away evil from your flesh'
and (Ps. 41.1): 'Happy is he that considers the poor, God will deliver
him from the day of evil.' 'Evil' here refers to the day of the judg-

ment, to *Gehennom*, as it is said, 'And the wicked for the day of evil,' and 'Happy are they that keep justice, that give charity at all times.' Why did our forefathers earn the right to this world, to the Messianic era, and to the world to come?—because they habituated themselves to giving charity. Abraham, Isaac and Jacob, Moses, Aaron, David and his son, Solomon, were praised only for their charity. From where do we learn concerning Abraham? — As it is said (Gen. 18.19): 'For I have known him to the end that he may command his children and his household after him that they shall keep the way of *Hashem*, to perform charity and justice.' Isaac was praised for his charity, as it is said (Gen. 26.12): 'And he sowed in that land. . .', and sowing indicates charity, as it is said (Hos. 10.12): 'Sow for yourselves in charity.' (The connection is that just as a man longs to sow his field, even though, at the time, he merely casts his seed on the ground—he is nevertheless confident that it will yield a hundredfold later on—so should one long to give charity, and be just as confident that God will repay many times over for the small loss of capital suffered at present, as it is said [Deut. 15.10]: 'You shall surely give. . .for on account of this thing God will bless you.") Jacob declared (Gen. 32.11): 'I have done too little to deserve all the benevolence and all the truth.' 'Little' here refers to charity, as it is said (Prov. 16.8): 'A little given in charity is better than great revenues acquired in injustice.' (Jacob declared that his accomplishments in charity were inadequate as compared with all the kindnesses 'You have done to Your servant.') As for Aaron and Moses, 'The Torah of truth was in his mouth' and 'truth' here indicates charity, as it is said (Ps. 85.12): 'Truth shall sprout from the ground and *tzedakah* shall look down from heaven.' David, as it is said (2 Sam. 8.15): 'And David executed justice and charity to all his people.' Solomon—(Ps. 72.1): 'And charity to the king's son! God, also, is praised through charity, as it is said (Is. 5.16): 'And God who is holy is sanctified through charity.' Even the Throne of Glory—(Ps. 89.15) 'Charity and justice are the foundations of Your throne.' Great is charity for it rescues man from the path of death, as Scripture asserts (Prov. 10.2): 'And charity shall rescue from death.'

"Come and see how man receives measure for measure. If a man gives charity in this world and intends thereby to preserve the life of the poor, to keep them from dying, the Holy One, blessed be He, wills that the donor should live and not die. And from where is it evident that whoever has the means to give charity and does not, to preserve life and does not, that he brings death upon himself? — From Nabal, who answered (1 Sam. 25.11): 'Shall I then take my bread and water. . .and give it to men whom I know not?' He was punished soon afterwards, as it is said (Ibid. 26.38): 'And God smote Nabal, so that he died.'

"Great is charity for it prolongs the days and years of man, as it is said (Deut. 30.20): 'For that is your life and the length of your days.' And it is stated too (Prov. 3.18): 'It is a tree of life to them that grasp it.' Now we may argue from premise to conclusion (*Kal Vachomer*): If for the very lightest of all mitzvoth it is promised (Deut. 22.27) 'So that it should be well with you that you may prolong your days,' how much more so is this true of charity, one of the most important mitzvoth of the Torah. Great is charity for it leads man to the world to come, as it is said (Ps. 1.1): '(*Ashrei*) Happy is the man that has not walked in the counsel of the wicked. . .', and also (Ps. 106.3) '(*Ashrei*) Happy are they that keep justice, that give charity at all times.' *Ashrei* (Happy) is used in connection with Torah, and also in connection with charity. Just as the *ashrei* referring to Torah assures life in the world to come, so does the *ashrei* referring to charity."

Great is charity for it is equal to Torah. Of Torah it is said (Lev. 26.8): 'If you will walk in My statutes,' and of charity (Prov. 8.22): 'God has made me as the beginning of His way.' Concerning Torah it is said (Lev. 26.6 ff.): 'And I will give peace in the land, and you shall lie down, and none shall make you afraid; and I will cause evil beasts to cease out of the land, neither shall the sword go through your land.' And of charity it is said (Isa. 32.17): 'And the work of charity shall be peace and the effect of charity quietness and confidence for ever. And My people shall abide in a peaceable habitation and in secure dwellings and in quiet resting-places.' Great is charity for the Torah has been compared and is equal to it, for there is no better creation in the world than Torah, as it is said (Prov. 4.8): 'Extol her and she will exalt you. She will bring you honor when you embrace her. She will give your head a chaplet of grace. A crown of glory she will bestow on you.' And Torah is compared to none other than charity, as it is said (Deut. 6.25): 'And it shall be a charity to us if we observe to do all this commandment.'

"Great indeed is charity for it hastens the advent of the Messianic era and the ultimate redemption, as it is said (Isa. 56.1): 'Keep justice and give charity, for My salvation is near to come and My charity to be revealed.'

"Great is charity for it exalts the soul and places it under the Throne of Glory, as it is said (Isa. 33.15): 'He that walks in charity and speaks uprightly...shall dwell on high, his place of defence shall be on the munitions of rocks, his bread shall be given, his water sure. Your eyes shall see the King in His beauty.' "

It is related in the *Avoth de R. Nathan* (Chap. 3): "There was once a *chasid* who was habitually charitable. One time he set out in a boat; a wind rose and sank his boat in the sea. R. Akiva witnessed this and came before the court to testify so that his wife might remarry. Before he could take the stand, the man came back and stood before him. Are you the one who went down in the sea? R. Akiva said to him. Yes, he replied. And who raised you out of the sea?—The charity which I practised, he answered, it raised me out of the sea. How do you know this?—R. Akiva inquired. He said to him: When I sank to the depths I heard the sound of a great noise of the waves of the sea, one wave saying to the other, and the other to another: Hurry, let us raise this man out of the sea for he practised charity all his days. Then R. Akiva spoke up and declared: Blessed be God, the God of Israel,Who has chosen the words of the Torah and the words of the sages, for the words of the Torah and the words of the sages are established for ever and to all eternity. For it is said (Eccl. 11.1): 'Cast your bread upon the waters, for you shall find it after many days' and (Prov. 10.2) 'Charity rescues from death.' "

For the merit of charity, blessing enters man's home, as it is said (Deut. 15.10): "You shall surely give him, and your heart shall not be grieved when you give unto him, because that for this thing *Hashem* your God will bless you in all your work."

Therefore every person should strive constantly to perform this mitzvah and thereby cause blessing to enter his home. This blessing is in addition to the everlasting reward that is stored away for him.

18

GIVING A TENTH TO CHARITY

Now we shall proceed to explain what one should do to fulfill at all times the requirements of the mitzvah of *chesed*. In the previous chapters we have demonstrated the desirability of setting aside a sum of money to be held in readiness for this mitzvah. One might find such a practice very difficult. He should, therefore, train himself to deduct a tenth from the total income God grants him. Of this amount, he should spend two thirds on charity gifts (the demand for which is the greater) and one third should be held in his possession for giving free loans. When a substantial sum has been accumulated, sufficient for the requests for loans, he should, from then on, allocate all his tithes for charity gifts alone.

The practice of tithing is most significant, as the *Gemara* indicates (Ta'anith 9): "Give a tithe (*'aser*), and you shall become enriched" (*tith'asher*). It is forbidden to put the Holy One, blessed be He, to the test, in any aspect of life. Only in respect of charity is this permitted, since Scripture has so declared (Mal. 3.10): "Bring the whole tithe into the store-house that there may be food in My house, and try me now herewith, says the God of Hosts, if I will not open for you the gates of heaven and pour you out a blessing that there shall be more than sufficiency." The *Yoreh Deah* renders the legal decision (Chap. 247) that in giving tithes it is permissible to test God, may He be blessed.

The requirements of giving the tenth (*ma'aser*) are fulfilled in this manner: One first sets aside one tenth of his capital. After that, whenever God grants him the opportunity and he acquires income, he should set aside one tenth of his earnings. Many allocate the tenth of their earnings, but not of their capital. They are not properly fulfilling the mitzvah as defined in the Codes. At first, one should deduct the tenth of his capital. Because of the multitude of our sins, however, the *yetzer harah* seizes control of man and does not allow him to give away his capital. One is therefore well advised to set aside the tenth of his capital for free loans to the poor. He can even lend this money to himself, when necessary, on the condition, however, that if he is meanwhile approached by someone in financial straits, he would have to borrow an amount equal to what he has taken from his own fund and advance it to the poor person. In this manner he will have fulfilled his *ma'aser* obligation, since such giving is also regarded as *tzedakah*, as we have explained above.

This method, however, is valid only in the view of the *Rambam* and the *Shulchan Aruch*. These authorities include loans to the poor in the category of *tzedakah*. The *Ramban*, however, in his notes on *Sefer Hamitzvoth*, does not classify this practice under *tzedakah*, but considers it a separate mitzvah. From his point of view, there is no proof that the mitzvah of *ma'aser* is fulfilled if the money will ultimately be restored to the donor or to his heirs. If, however, when one first undertakes to observe the mitzvah, he explicitly stipulates that he will devote this money to an irrevocable Free Loan Fund, then, certainly, this would be permissible according to the *Rambam* and the *Shulchan Aruch*, and even the *Ramban's* view would, apparently, allow a lenient interpretation.

All that we have written applies to the person wishing to reserve his *ma'aser* sums for loans and not for outright gifts to the poor. However, if he wishes to lend *ma'aser* money he has set aside, for a period of time, to a rich man, certainly to those temporarily in straitened circumstances, or to the permanently poor, but he intends to pay the equivalent sum, if and when a worthy poor person presents himself, then there is no need at all to follow the stricter ruling, even according to the *Ramban's* opinion, as is explained in *Yoreh Deah* (Chap. 258, Par. 1). I subsequently found, with God's help, that *Eliyahu Rabbah* (Chap. 156) too has ruled explicitly that to grant a free loan from *ma'aser* money even to a man of means is permissible, the intention of the lender being that this is for a temporary period, until a poor person applies for a loan.

We shall now resume our discussion, and to some extent explain how a person should deal with *ma'aser* money. To avoid all pitfalls, he should make the following stipulations: (a) When he first undertakes to fulfill the mitzvah, he should declare that he is not binding himself by any vow. This will prevent him inadvertently being guilty at times, Heaven forbid, of committing this transgression. (b) He should keep a special account book in which he enters all the net earnings (after deducting his business expenses) which God has granted him. He should balance his accounts semi-annually, or at least annually. If he has incurred any losses, Heaven forbid, during this period, he should deduct these amounts from his earnings, and the remainder should form the basis for calculating the *ma'aser*. (c) During the entire period, he should enter all the sums he dispensed as charity. Any amount given in his house to the poor may also be included, even if it is only a penny. All these amounts should be deducted from the *ma'aser*. (d) If at the time of balancing his account he sees that the *ma'aser* exceeds the amounts dispensed, he should immediately set aside the difference and distribute it. If the poor to whom he will give the money are not at hand, he may retain the balance of his *ma'aser* until they come. In the meantime, he may use the money for his own purposes. When, however, those poor persons to whom he gives approach him, he will be obliged to borrow and give them the money at once. (e) If he discovers that his charity donations exceed his *ma'aser* allocations, some authorities allow him to carry the balance forward to the next year. Others render a stricter ruling. Hence it is advisable to follow the procedure we recommend: to stipulate expressly when he first undertakes to perform this mitzvah that he may reimburse himself from his *ma'aser* money for any charity donations he may make, at any time he may desire.

Such procedures are possible for people whose profits are obtained in lump sums at intervals. It is almost impossible for a storekeeper, however, to record the minute profit he earns on each individual sale. For him the practice recommended is to appraise, generally, the gain in his inventory and his accounts receivable. Thus he would calculate his net income. Then he should make a general estimate of his household expenses for food and clothing for the period involved. Against the total of these two items, he should add up all his charity donations and include all sums dispensed in his house. He should also stipulate, when he first undertakes to fulfill this mitzvah, that he be permitted to rely on his own estimates, and not be required to calculate precisely.

One is also required to distribute a tenth of any inheritance he may become heir to (*Eliyahu Rabba* Chap. 156).

19

LAWS CONCERNING THE DISTRIBUTION OF A TENTH
OR A FIFTH TO CHARITY

Now we shall deal with the manner in which the *ma'aser* money is to be distributed. Basically, of course, the money is to be given as charity to the poor. Poor relatives take precedence over strangers. (For the rules of priority, consult *Yoreh Deah*, Chap. 351, Par. 3.) One may even allocate sums to his older children whom he is no longer obliged to support. Since they have not their own means, the amounts given them are certainly charity gifts, even if the father is able to provide for them from other sources. A poor man may even support his father and mother from these funds. If, however, he is able to provide for them from other sources, then the declaration of *Chazal* would apply to him: "Let a curse fall on whoever supports his father and mother out of charity funds." (See *Yoreh Deah*, Chaps. 240, 249. *Shach* ibid.)

If his own relatives are not in need, and he distributes his charity money among others, he should by right endeavor first and foremost to allocate the sums to those "who labor in Torah," since the Midrash (*Tanchuma Re'eh*) indicates that this type of *ma'aser* was first instituted for the support of those preoccupied with Torah study. Here is the relevant passage: " 'You shall surely (*'aser*) give a tithe (*te'aser*).' Give a tithe thereby to become wealthy; give a tithe and thereby you will suffer no lack. This is an intimation to those who 'span the seas' (engage in business) that they should set aside a tenth for those who labor in the Torah." Scripture also promises that

163

one's household will be blessed, as it is said (Mal. 3.10): "Bring all the whole tithe into the storehouse that there may be food in My house, and try Me now herewith, says the God of Hosts, if I will not open for you the windows of heaven and pour you out a blessing that there will be more than sufficiency." The intent here is that, being given food in "God's house", the Priests and Levites will be able to devote themselves to the study of God's Torah, and on this account God's blessing of abundance will be granted, for "the blessing follows immediately after the *Talmid Chacham*," as *Chazal* have asserted (Berachoth 42a). (In similar vein they have declared [Chullin 130b]: "Portions are not given to ignorant Priests, as it is said [2 Chron. 31.4]: 'To give the portions of the Priests and Levites that they might devote themselves to the Torah of God.' ") If one is unable to distribute the entire sum among students of Torah, he should give them the major portion or, at least, a half. I have found this ruling in the *Knesseth Hagedolah* (*Yoreh Deah*, Chap. 249, Par. 1, q.v.). The same is evident from the remarks of Harav Hame'ili (*Shittah Mekubetzeth*, Kethuvoth 50a) that the present *ma'aser* is patterned after the tithes given to the Priests and Levites for them to devote themselves to the Torah of God.

You should know that the later authorities (*Acharonim*) have ruled that the *ma'aser* money may be used to enable groom and bride to marry, if they could not do so otherwise. This also applies to the arranging of a *brith milah* or the purchasing of *sefarim* to be lent to others. One is also permitted to use these volumes for his own study, but he must take care to inscribe that the works have been purchased with *ma'aser* money. Otherwise his sons may take possession of them as their own property after his death. Others doubt the legality of such practices. The *Pithchei Teshuvah* (citing the *Chatham Sofer*, Yoreh Deah Chap. 249) states that the Maharil and Rama only allow the *Ma'aser* money to be given to the poor, and not to be used for any other mitzvah-purpose. If, however, it is evident that his participation in the expenses of the *brith* benefits the child's father, who is poor and cannot afford the cost, and that the bride and groom, and those for whom he purchases the books, are all poor, then there is no reason to follow the stricter opinion in this instance, since such contributions really constitute charity gifts. As for buying the right to be called to the Torah, if here too the money goes towards helping the poor, there is no reason to rule against one's using this money, according to all the authorities. All legal opinions, however, forbid the use of these funds to pay for the Torah tuition of his own children, since he is personally obliged to teach them himself, or else to hire a tutor for them, and he is forbidden to pay his personal debts with *ma'aser* money. To defray the tuition of the children of other poor people is certainly permitted. It is a great mitzvah.

You should know too, that the giving of one tenth to charity is the practice for the average person. Whoever wishes to act generously, however, should set apart one fifth of his possessions. *Chazal* have found support for this idea in Scripture (Gen. 28.22): "And of all that You give me, a tenth—a tenth will I give. . ."—twice one tenth equalling one fifth. Here too, I believe, one is first to give a fifth of his net worth and then one fifth of all his subsequent earnings. In distributing the funds, one should divide them into two: one tenth going to students of the Torah (corresponding to the first tithe given to the Priests and Levites to devote themselves to the study of the Torah, as Scripture has stated), and the second tenth for mitzvah purposes. So I have learned from the *Shittah Mekubetzeth* (Kethuvoth 50a) quoting Harav Hameili.

Now we shall explain a matter which especially affects the giving of charity. Some authorities declare that *Chazal* have only regarded the contribution of one fifth to be the characteristic of the generous, when there are no cases of poor people who have no food or clothes. However, if it is known that there are widows, orphans and the like, the oppressed who are unable to help themselves, then one is duty bound, *by law*, to set aside one fifth of one's possessions. This is the opinion of the Vilna Gaon, as is evident from his writings. This obligation arises only where the donor is capable of contributing such a proportion of his possessions. However, one is not obliged by law to endure hardship in order to give this second tenth though it is a mitzvah to do so, as we have written above (and we have elaborated our view in the note in the Hebrew edition).

20

DETAILS RELATING TO PROFUSE SPENDING
ON CHARITY

According to the Gemara (Kethuvoth 50a), the Sages in Usha instituted that the profuse spender on charity should not distribute more than a fifth, lest he thereby later become dependent on public support. This admonition does not refer to the extremely wealthy person, according to the authorities, since he was expressly excluded from the ordinance. (See: Bava Kamma 9b, Tosafoth s.v. *Ilema*; also, *Chochmath Adam*, Laws of Charity.) Nor does it include the critically ill who makes a distribution immediately prior to his death. The reservation that he might become dependent on charity does not apply; therefore, he may give away a larger amount. (In his note on Yoreh Deah, Chap. 249, Par. 1, Rama rules that such a person may dispose of as much as he wishes. (Cf. the later authorities who cite the opinion that such a person may give away one third or a half of his wealth, but not more.) The Gemara relates of Mar Ukva (Kethuvoth 67b) that he reviewed the sums he had distributed in his lifetime, and remarked, "The way is long and the provisions scanty." He thereupon allocated one half of his possessions to charity.

Some authorities declare that the rule, "the generous giver shall not give away more than a fifth," only applies when the donor seeks, of his own volition, to find needy people and to distribute charity among them. When, however, hungry and bare individuals approach him, whom he is duty bound to feed and clothe as the Torah requires (Deut. 15.8): "Sufficient for his needs in which he is lacking," or, if

167

he were to encounter captives to whom the Divinely ordained obligation to redeem applies, then, if he wished to spend more than a fifth of his capital for this purpose, he is permitted, and this is deemed a saintly characteristic (Rambam: Mishnah Commentary, *Peah*, Chap. 1). Apparently the limitation does not apply where danger to life is involved. If, for instance, the captive is in danger of his life or the hungry of starving to death, then the limit of one fifth is inoperative. The Gemara (Bava Metzia 62a) only lays down that one's own life takes priority over his neighbor's; we have found no source to indicate that one's wealth takes precedence over his neighbor's life.

Know, too, that the injunction limiting one's spending to one fifth only applies when one squanders his possessions. This is indicated by the term *mevazbez*. Where a person holds a steady position or owns a going concern from which he derives his weekly sustenance and a little more besides, he is allowed to spend the extra income on charity even if, proportionately, this amounts to more than one fifth of his earnings.

Know, further, that the ordinance as such refers only to charity in general. As for the support of Torah learning, the *Shittah Mekubetzeth* takes the view that this is not included in the restriction. This is logical, since the donor receives a share of the reward for the Torah study, as we find in the case of Issachar and Zevulun. The tribe of Zevulun supported the tribe of Issachar and took a share in the reward for their Torah study. We find the Midrash stating (Bamidbar Rabba, *Nasso*, 13.17): "Why was Zevulun privileged to offer his sacrifice third in the order of the princes? Because he loved Torah. He generously gave his money to Issachar to free the latter from having to engage in trade. Hence Issachar did not need to interrupt his preoccupation with Torah. Zevulun thereby achieved the merit of becoming Issachar's partner and associate in his Torah... Another interpretation: The 'silver dish' corresponded to the bread which he (Zevulun) fed him (Issachar); the 'basin' to the wine he gave him to drink; and why were these articles made of silver—to indicate that he gave him money to cover all his needs. 'Both were filled with fine flour' teaches that both together received the reward for Torah and a common sustenance...for just as Zevulun shared in Issachar's reward for Torah, so Issachar shared in Zevulun's material gains." This passage makes it evident that the support granted to Issachar far exceeded one fifth. *Chazal* have, many times, cited the behavior of Issachar and Zevulun as the example to be followed by succeeding generations. How can we claim, then, that this is impossible for our generation? Obviously, cases where Torah support is involved are not bound to this limitation. Since the reward is shared, how could there be any limitation? The greater the measure of support, the greater the share of the reward. (Note: The person who fears God intelligently will be able to discover from this Midrash how he should conduct himself in this joint enterprise. When the *Talmid Chacham* comes to him he should cordially welcome the former, as if his business partner, whose association with him yields large profits, were meeting him. For supporting the *Talmid Chacham* gladly, he will ultimately receive his due reward in the world to come. Some boorish individuals, because of our many sins, behave otherwise. They give their contributions in a niggardly, grudging and humiliating manner. Man is repaid, Heaven forfend, for such conduct, measure for measure. "As for the wise man, his eyes are in his head.")

In its exposition of the verse (Eccl. 2.18): "So I hated all my labor," the Midrash (Koheleth Rabba, ad loc.) relates: "R. Meir was a skillful scribe and used to earn three *selas* a week. He spent one *sela* on food and drink, another on clothing and the third on *Talmidei Chachamim*. His disciples asked him: What will you leave for your children? He answered: If they are righteous, then it will be as David said (Ps. 37.25): 'Yet I have not seen the righteous forsaken nor his seed begging bread.' And if they are not righteous, why should I leave my possessions to enemies of the Allpresent?" The Midrash further remarks (Eccl. 7.11): "R. Acha said in the name of

R. Tanchum: Suppose one had studied, taught, kept and observed the Torah. He could also have afforded to support others (who study Torah) but did not. He is then included in the category of (Deut. 27.26) 'Cursed be he who does not uphold the words of this Torah.' Suppose, again, that one had neither studied nor taught, neither observed nor kept the Torah. (The intent here is that his devotion to Torah was impaired by his poverty and cares. He was hard pressed to earn his daily living, as the concluding words bear out, 'was unable.') He was unable to afford to, yet helped others, then he falls in the category of 'Blessed be he who upholds the words of this Torah.' "

From all that has been said, the greatness of the importance of supporting Torah even when one earns a meager living becomes apparent. The person will be blessed for his deeds. How much more should one exert himself in performing this mitzvah when his means are ample.

We revert to our discussion. The limitation imposed by *Chazal* shows how carefully we should reflect and guard against squandering money on worthless trifles. Obviously, charity and other mitzvoth are the supremely important of all activities in the world. Expenditures of such items rescue the giver from suffering, both in this world and the next. Yet our Sages have warned us to be sparing, not to spend too much on such matters lest we become impoverished, even though God might by miraculous means provide for us in such an instance. How much more should one take care not to spend his money on follies, such as honor, which is specious, dressing gaudily, living in lavish mansions, employing many servants, using the most expensive household utensils. Such expenditures deplete man's wealth in a short space of time and lead him to poverty. He then comes to engage in dishonest dealing, disrespecting the property of others, because of his own straitened condition.

Now I know well the arguments advanced by one's inclinations, that living on a high standard increases one's capacity to earn profits, since people will take him to be rich and will extend him large credits. This too is absurd. Everyone sees through his deceit. His affairs are investigated and the truth uncovered. Of necessity, then, all his previous expenditures will have been in vain. Furthermore, his sons and daughters, seeing his extravagant living, truly believe that their father is extremely wealthy. They squander his money even more recklessly on all kinds of worthless things. Finally he is reduced to penury. His downfall is fully exposed. Creditors keep surrounding and dunning him. The resulting pain and shame almost threatens his life and the lives of his entire household. Instead of the imaginary, fleeting happiness which deluded them at first, they now suffer long and enduring degradation and heartache. The wise man will accordingly be forewarned not to dissipate his wealth on worthless matters. He will spend only for necessities, charity and *gemiluth chesed*. Then all will be well with him.

I intend to raise one more point. Those who adopt the practice of setting aside one-tenth or one-fifth of all their earnings perform a much greater deed than those who give without assuming the obligation, even if the amounts in both cases turn out to be the same. The latter fulfill the mitzvah of *tzedakah* only. The former, however, form a partnership with Heaven, and so their commercial activities as such have the advantage of being a mitzvah. This applies especially when, at the time of assuming the *ma'aser* or one-fifth obligation, the person had in mind that God would be sharing in all his undertakings. How goodly is his portion and how pleasant his lot.

21

PROVIDING SUPPORT TO FORESTALL COLLAPSE

So far we have dealt with the normal *gemiluth chesed* that benefits one's neighbor, poor or rich. Now we shall discuss another subdivision of this class. Someone's financial condition has deteriorated. With the loan extended to him, he is able to maintain himself, to save himself from collapse and dependence on others. This support is greater than the ordinary type of *gemiluth chesed*, for here one also fulfills the Scriptural command (Lev. 25.35): "And if your brother be waxen poor, then you shall uphold him; even if he be a stranger and a settler, he shall live with you." (As for the Scriptural expression, "with you", this can be explained by reference to the verse [Prov. 22.2]: "The rich and the poor meet together; God is the Maker of them all," as expounded by *Chazal*. "When the poor approaches the rich and says, 'Support me,' then if the latter does support him, well and good. If not, 'God is the Maker of them all'—He who made this one rich can make him poor..." So when a poor person approaches you, you should imagine that you yourself had become financially unstable, since, if you do not help him, your security too, might, God forbid, collapse. If, however, you help him to stabilize his position, both of you will live and endure. This is the meaning of "and he shall live with you.") Now if God grants the beneficiary some profit through this loan and he earns a livelihood for his household and himself, then God will regard the lender as having preserved the life of the borrower and his family. So we have explained previously on the authority of the Midrash.

172

If one finds some employment for him in industry or service, this, too, will fall within the scope of the mitzvah, as is found in the Rambam's Code. The rule is that one should exert himself to the fullest extent to save the next person from financial collapse. One should do whatever one can, since sometimes, by merely encouraging others to do something for him, one assists this person in his affairs. I have seen God-fearing individuals lend money to such people as free loans and then allow the debtors to repay in weekly installments, instead of all at once. They do these unfortunates a great favor, since the debtor can repay the loan and still maintain his economic independence. It would be different if the debtor was pressed to repay the entire amount in one lump sum. He would be reduced to his previous poverty.

We find this topic discussed in the Gemara (Avodah Zarah 4a): "He who lends his neighbor 1,000 *zuz* shall, if he loves him, allow him to repay a little at a time." One should follow the example of business practice. The creditors allow their debtors this courtesy, so their money is preserved and profits thereby increased. So should one behave with these distressed souls by granting them free loans, thereby properly to perform God's will. The good name, with which God will crown the donor in the world to come on this account, will obtain greater honor for him than the insignificant profits the money lender gains in his transactions. (So the Gemara [Shabbath 104a] asserts: "Learn wisdom; show kindness to the poor...and if you do this, the Holy One blessed be He will sustain you...and bind a crown on you in the world to come." Apparently this is the meaning of Avoth [4.13]: "And the crown of a good name is better than all.")

Whoever acts in this manner fulfills the words of the verse (Ps. 41.1): "Happy is he who considers the poor. God will deliver him in the day of evil." The verse praises his consideration of the circumstances and degradation of the poor, his effort to see whether he can to some extent extricate the poor from his penury and need. This verse has many other ramifications, as we shall, please God, explain further on, and what we have said here also falls within its scope.

The worthy conduct we have described does not only include loans granted by individuals, but public *gemiluth chesed* activities as well. I have seen several communities where such holy societies, conducted in this manner, have recently been established. These organizations bear the name *Somech Nofelim*, since they support the poor and prevent them from collapsing [God forbid]. They proceed in this manner. They advance a certain sum specified in their by-laws for a stipulated period of time. The burden of repayment is lightened by the borrower returning a small amount each week. The guardians of the fund appoint an honorary or paid official who goes to the borrowers to collect their weekly installments, so the treasury is hardly ever depleted. This procedure also confers an added advantage. At the time the loan is made, the mitzvah of "and you shall strengthen him" is fulfilled. This is the primary virtue of the mitzvah of *tzedakah*, as the Code of the *Rambam* and the *Yoreh Deah* (Chap. 249) explain. In addition, at the time of repayment, *chesed* is manifested, since the debtor is treated with kindness. *Chazal's* remark is well known (Sukkah 49b): "R. Eliezer said: Charity is rewarded in proportion to the *chesed* it manifests."

Know, too, that the *Yoreh Deah* (Chap. 249) rules that a gift which stabilizes a person's financial condition when he is on the verge of collapse is also a fulfillment of this mitzvah. So when a misfortune befalls a person (the animal with which he plies his trade dies, or similar cases of loss) and he cannot himself replace the loss — or when a woman becomes widowed and unable to support herself, and if she is granted a sum of money, she will be able to engage in some occupation, great care should be taken to help them. All acts of this type are a great mitzvah. Long life is granted in recompense, as the Midrash explains in expounding the verse (Prov. 19.17): "He that is gracious to the poor lends to God". A similar case is found in Bava Bathra (11a), in the incident involving Benjamin the righteous.

Know further, that the provision of gainful employment, or similar assistance to the poor, fulfills the mitzvah of "And you shall uphold him," according to the legal authorities. This is an open reprimand to those who are not particular in giving the employment to a Jew when they require unskilled labor. These workers are certainly not rich. They are almost paupers. The verse (Lev. 25.35): "And if your brother be waxen poor" certainly describes their circumstances. Furthermore, even where the man is known to be rich, and is not referred to by this verse, nevertheless, as a Jew he takes priority over a non-Jew, in buying from him, selling to him, and the like. So we find in the *Sifra*. Know too, that the *Rama* in his Responsa (Chap. 6) rules that even where there is a slight difference in price, a Jew is to be preferred to a non-Jew, and we have transcribed his remarks (Part I, Chap. 5, Par. 6). He refers to any Jew, and the same certainly applies to a poor laborer to whom the mitzvah of "And you shall uphold him" refers. So the law certainly appears to be, as explained above.

A person should put his trust in God. He should believe that for the mitzvah of "And you shall uphold him", the highest form of *tzedakah* (Yoreh Deah, Chap. 249), God will cause him to prosper in the home he is building or on the journey he undertakes, besides reserving the due reward for him in the world to come. We have described to the reader the many ways in which this "upholding" can be accomplished. The wise will be able to make the proper application to all relevant situations. He should, also, realize that the mitzvah is not fulfilled once and for all by any single act. Every time someone needs support to save him from collapse, he must be helped. So the Midrash explains (Sifra, *Behar*): "Even if you have upheld him four or five times, uphold him once more, since Scripture declares, 'And you shall uphold him.' " (A similar deduction is made [Sifrei, Deut. 15.8]: " 'You shall open, open your hand'—even many times are meant.")

22

GEMILUTH CHESED IN LENDING CHATTELS, ETC.

In the previous chapters we have expounded the laws of lending money. Now we shall deal with chattels. This activity, too, stems from compassion and constitutes a mitzvah, as *Chazal* have pointed out (Sukkah 49b): "Charity is performed with one's money; *chesed* with one's money and one's self." Rashi explains *chesed* here to mean the lending of money, chattels, livestock — all being included in the mitzvah. And the mitzvah is all the greater if, through the loan of the article or animal, the borrower will be able to earn his means of livelihood. Certainly this is a most important deed, for the lender fulfills the Scriptural admonition (Lev. 25.35): "And if your brother be waxen poor and his means fail with you, then you shall uphold him . . ." Everyone is capable of performing this type of *chesed,* since even small articles, household utensils, or a comb would be included. And *Chazal* have declared that the punishment is greater for laxity in respect of the white threads of the *tzitzith* than of the blue (*techeleth*). The blue threads are expensive; not everyone can afford them; not so with regard to the white. The same comparison applies to our case. In heaven, no demands will be made of a person in financial straits for having failed to lend a friend the substantial sum the friend would need to support himself. Yet one will be brought to account for the small article which he could have lent to, and so helped, his neighbor — yet he did not do so, because of his laziness. So in our matter. Every person can give his neighbor the benefit of these small items. Even if the person seeking such a favor were wealthy, one would be obliged to extend him this courtesy. How much more is one certainly obliged to lend such articles to a poor person, since the latter might not be able to afford their purchase, as we have explained above (ch. 1) in the Laws of Lending (*Nethiv Hachesed, q.v.*). Now, there are even some people who, though not using the article at the time, refuse to lend it because of their parsimony. They begrudge the use of their possessions to others. How despicable is this trait. We have already explained (in Chap. 11) how ugly it is and what punishment it entails. Again, even those who are not by nature niggardly often fail to lend out their possessions because of sheer laziness (the article, for instance, lies in another room) or for some other trivial reason. Even though the latter are not included in the first category, nevertheless their souls have never been illuminated by the glow of *chesed*, and they have no conception of its significance. Were they to realize its great value, they would allow nothing to interfere with their exercise of this virtue in all their affairs. They would rejoice whenever the Almighty granted them an opportunity to be good and compassionate towards their fellow men.

So far, we have directed our attention to the lending of utensils and other articles which only provide temporary benefit. How much more does one accomplish by lending *sefarim* to his friend for study. He thereby confers everlasting benefit upon his friend. His own merit and righteousness will endure for ever, as *Chazal* have asserted in reference to the verse (Ps. 112.3): "Wealth and riches are in his house; and his merit endures forever" — "this is the person who writes *sefarim* and lends them out to others." This act also constitutes the mitzvah of "upholding the Torah" for which one receives blessing from God, may He be blessed, as *Chazal* have stated.

Some refrain from lending their possessions because of some slight antipathy they harbor against the borrower. This is the worst of all the vices mentioned above. Here, one transgresses the prohibition (Lev. 19.18): "You shall not take vengeance or bear any grudge against the children of your people." We have already previously dealt at length with this topic (Part I, Chap. 4, q. v.). One should rather pay regard to himself, recalling how many times he provoked the Holy One, blessed be He, both in word and by deed. Nevertheless the Holy One, blessed be He, does not take revenge or bear any grudge against him in any of his dealings. One should, therefore, act in the same way towards his neighbor. We may assert that this is the intent of the verse (Lev. 19.18): "You shall not take vengeance ... but you shall love your neighbor as yourself ; I am God." You shall extend towards your neighbor the virtues I extend towards you and towards the world as a whole, since I do not bear any hatred, as is stated (Jer. 3.12): "For I am merciful, says God, I will not bear a grudge forever."

We have so far directed our remarks to the lender; now we shall discuss the borrower. He must beware not to break the terms stipulated by the lender. If he does, he is termed a *gazlan* (robber). He may not use the borrowed article for any purpose not stipulated, nor may he retain it beyond the allotted time. So too, anyone who takes something belonging to another person and uses it without the owner's consent is called a robber, as is laid down in the *Choshen Mishpat* (Chap. 341 and 359). The borrower is further prohibited from lending the article to anyone else, even during the period of the loan, and certainly not after the expiration. He is responsible to return the article to the owner when the period of the loan ends. Many people, because of our many sins, are careless in this instance; they are too lazy to go and return the article. In the meantime the owner forgets who borrowed it, and he has to go about trying to discover the latter's identity. Frequently, too, the article is broken through the borrower's neglect. Even if he pays for it, this is still an injustice. The lender did not, in the first place, give him the article for such a purpose. If he fails to compensate for the loss, he is guilty of outright robbery, as the *Gemara* lays down (Bava Metzia 81a): "A borrower is legally bound to guard the article, even after the expiration of the period for which it was taken, as long as it still remains in his possession." He is certainly all the more liable during the specified period, even if the article was broken accidentally. Hence anyone concerned for his soul will act in this way when he borrows any article from his neighbor for any particular use. He will return it just as soon as he has finished using it, and will not retain it any longer. (See the *Shittah Mekubetzeth,* Bava Metzia 81a. There it is stated on the authority of the Ritva that the borrower is legally obliged to restore the article to the owner's possession as soon as the period for which it was borrowed expires.)

23

HOW TO ACT IN LENDING

In the previous chapters, we have explained in detail the obligation of lending to others. Now we shall proceed to demonstrate how this mitzvah is to be performed. One is required to behave in the same way as in giving charity. One should give the loan graciously and not with ill humor. So we find in *Avoth de R. Nathan* (Chap. 13): "And receive all persons with a cheerful countenance." What is that? This teaches that if a person gave all the gifts in the world to his neighbor, but his countenance is irritably downcast, Scripture regards him as not having given anything." This is the ruling in the *Yoreh Deah* (Chap. 249, Par. 3). The same applies to loans. One should beware not to subject the borrower to any indignity, Heaven forbid, but lend to him cheerfully. (See above, Chap. 9, where we have explained the matter thoroughly.) He should consider himself. Suppose he wanted to obtain a favor from his neighbor. How ardently would he wish his neighbor to receive him graciously. He should act the same way towards his neighbor. So Rashi has commented on the verse (Exod. 22.24): "If you lend money to My people, to the poor that is with you, you shall not treat him disrespectfully when lending him money, since he is "My people." "The poor that is with you" — look at yourself as if you were the poor man.

One must act especially gracious if the person has grown poor, and the granting of a loan will enable him to engage in gainful occupation whereby he will be saved from financial collapse and dependence on others. According to the *Rambam* and the *Shulchan*

Aruch (Yoreh Deah, Chap. 249), this act is included in the mitzvah of *tzedakah*, so one is certainly obliged to behave as in giving charity, as we have previously shown.

Hence, if for some reason or other, the person approached is unable to grant the loan, he must behave as in the case of charity (Chap. 249). He should not rebuke the applicant or raise his voice in talking to him, as do the niggardly, who not only refuse to help but also revile the poor for having knocked at their door. He should speak gently to the person, show that he really wishes to make the loan, but is presently prevented by adverse circumstances. The rule is: in the same way that he would want his neighbor to deal with him, so he should act towards his neighbor, as Rashi has set down in the quoted passage. And *Avoth de R. Nathan* continues: "Whoever receives a neighbor with a cheerful countenance (even if he gave him naught) is regarded by Scripture as if he gave him all the gifts in the world."

Now we shall explain how the mitzvah is to be performed for its own sake, without any ulterior motives. *Chazal* have stated (Pesachim 8a): "If someone says: I give this *sela* to charity that my son may live or that I may merit the world to come — he is completely righteous in this act" (Rashi). The same applies wherever one expects, also, to derive some benefit. The reason is that the person has obeyed God's will in saying that he gives the coin to charity. Even though he also desired to derive some benefit, his mitzvah is not nullified. Obviously the same principle applies to acts of *gemiluth chesed*. If a person sets aside a sum of money for *gemiluth chesed* loans or actually makes the loan, and at the same time he has in mind that his sons should be granted life on that account, or that he should prosper in business, or that he should merit the world to come, nevertheless his mitzvah is regarded as complete, since he fully intended to perform the mitzvah ordained by the Torah, but also wished that God, may He be blessed, grant him some favor in return. (This assertion does not contradict the accepted ruling of the *Orach*

Chaim [Chap. 60] that mitzvoth require intention — i.e. that one should intend to perform the act as a mitzvah. Here he does have in mind to perform a mitzvah. He only desires, *in addition,* that God grant him a boon for this act. Hence the mitzvah is complete.) would be better for him to perform the mitzvah for the sake of fulfilling God's Torah commandment only. Then the holy power of the mitzvah which has been performed in the most perfect manner possible will so strongly draw forth the Heavenly attribute of *chesed* that it will extend over all created existence.

Now a person may find himself incapable of performing a mitzvah for its own sake alone. His intention is always to benefit himself, that he should succeed in his affairs, be highly regarded in the community as a giver of charity and a doer of good deeds. He should nevertheless not abstain from performing the mitzvah on that account. The *Gemara* declares (Pesachim 50b): "Let a man always engage in Torah and mitzvoth, even if he has ulterior motives, since through acting with these ulterior motives he will come to engage in Torah and mitzvoth for their own sake." (See Rashi and Tosafoth, Berachoth 17a). Such acts also evoke Divine grace on the creation, though not over its entirety, but only as far as the heavens, as the *Gemara* points out (Pesachim 50b): "One verse reads (Ps. 57.11): 'For Your *chesed* is great unto the heavens.' Another (Ps. 108.5): 'For Your *chesed* is great above the heavens.' There is no contradiction. One refers to those who perform the mitzvah for its own sake, the other to where it is performed with ulterior motives." The *Gemara* (Bava Bathra 9a), which points out, "Nevertheless it is considered *tzedakah*" (Cf. ibid.), proves that regardless of the manner in which the act is performed, Scripture regards it as *tzedakah*, and the same applies to *chesed.* As *Chazal* have stated (Sifrei, *Ki Thetzeh*): "Even if someone lost a *sela* and it was found by a poor man, the All-present credits the loser with merit."

The Midrash *Tadsheh* (Chap. 12) explains: "There are three types of sacrifices: burnt, peace and sin offerings. There are three ways in

which the righteous serve: through love, supplication, and fear. The
burnt offering corresponds to love; the peace offering to supplication; the sin offering to fear. The burnt offering is brought for the
glory of God alone, but the peace and sin offerings for our personal
benefit. Love is the most precious. There are the righteous who serve
God in love and give honor and glory to His kingdom. For He alone
preserves everything; He, in His great goodness, created the world at
His word, without toil. He is God, the Father, the King, the Mighty,
Wise, Good, the Merciful, Who bears all, and Who has filled
everything, the upper and lower regions. He sustains His creatures,
knows the secrets of the world, does good to the righteous and the
wicked, and allows the wicked to endure that they may repent and
live. For all this good the righteous love the Allpresent, accord Him
praise and laudation for all His great deeds. And for this they bring
the burnt offering."

"What is the supplication?—There are those who worship God by
laying their supplications and requests before Him. They ask for all
manner of good things for themselves, such as wisdom and understanding, knowledge, long life, health, an intelligent wife, children of
good character, success, wealth, honor, prosperity, etc. This is "supplication." In this service peace offerings are brought.

"Now this is the method of fear: There are those who worship
God in great fear and trepidation. They pray to be rescued, both in
this world and the next, from the curses pronounced in Scripture
against those who betray His mitzvoth and who transgress the commandments of the Allpresent. They plead to be rescued in this world
from illness, pain and suffering, that they not become dependent on
others, that strangers should not rule them, that they should not see
their children die or suffer harm, and that their lives be filled with
good and blessing, that they be delivered (in the world to come) from
punishment and destruction and from the burning fires of *Gehennom*
which are destined to sear and consume the wicked on the great day
of judgment. This is the service of fear, in which a sin offering is
brought.

"Yet the three sacrifices, the burnt, peace and sin offerings, are brought in the same Temple by a single Cohen to One God, and all have equal significance. So the righteous who serve either through love, supplication or fear, shelter equally in the shadow of the Holy One, blessed be He. The one serving in love expresses his love for Him; the one who serves in supplication beseeches Him; the one who serves in fear, fears Him."

So here you have it explained. Even though each type has its own level, and the attribute of love is the most precious of all, nevertheless all are cherished by God, may He be blessed, since the peace and sin offerings are also said to give "an odor pleasing to *Hashem.*"

We may now argue our own case. Charity and *chesed,* in whatever form they are practised, are precious to God, may He be blessed. One must, however, take care to avoid performing charity and *chesed* to glorify himself over others afterwards, for then one destroys his mitzvah altogether. Each person should realize that all he possesses comes from the Holy One, blessed be He, as it is written (1 Chron. 29.14): "For all things come from You, and from Your own we have given to You."

24

THE IMPORTANCE OF REPAYING DEBTS

All this time, we have described the greatness of the mitzvah of making loans. Now we shall explain the importance of the obligation resting on the borrower to repay the loan. *Chazal* have declared (Kethuvoth 86a): "To repay a creditor is a mitzvah." One can as little evade this obligation as the observance of *Sukkah, Shofar, Tefillin* (Cf. ibid.). They have furthermore asserted (Bava Metzia 114a) that food for thirty days, clothes for twelve months, not more, and the tools of the debtor are exempted from distraint, when the lender is empowered by the Beth Din to seize the recalcitrant debtor's possessions. All the rest of his immovable and movable property, his books etc. are sold to defray what he owes. Nothing is held back for the feeding of his wife and children. His creditor holds a lien over all he possesses.

As for one who refuses to pay (he has the means but is powerful enough to resist), he transgresses the explicit injunction of the Torah (Lev. 19.13): "You shall not oppress your neighbor." As is laid down in the *Choshen Mishpat* (Chap. 359, Par. 8): "What constitutes oppression? — A person gains possession of his neighbor's money with the owner's consent. When payment is demanded, he retains his neighbor's money by force and refuses to return it. For instance, someone was owed a debt or his wages. He demands the money, but is unable to exact payment because the defendant retains the money by force." *Chazal* have also designated four types of persons as wicked, and one is the borrower who does not repay, as it is said (Ps.

185

37.21): "The wicked borrows, and does not repay." How ashamed should a person feel when he knows he can repay, but does not, and thereby attaches the name of *rasha'* to himself. Now if his neighbor were to call him *rasha'*, even in private when he would suffer no embarassment, he would nevertheless greatly resent the insult. How much shame will he eventually suffer in the future, when his notoriety will be exposed in the presence of myriads upon myriads of holy beings. So the holy books have stated, that all man's affairs are disclosed and made public in everyone's presence in Heaven. He may be able to assume an impressive appearance towards his contemporaries, acting as if he were innocent, but to God the greatness of his crime is revealed.

This is what *Chazal* meant by saying (Avoth 2.13): "And do not be wicked in your own esteem." (Especially if one is a *Talmid Chacham* is his sin exceedingly grave, for he desecrates the Divine Name. Beside his other wrongs, he transgresses the prohibition (Lev. 22.32): "And do not profane My holy Name." *Chazal* have given the matter even greater emphasis (Yoma 87): "How is His Name desecrated? — If one buys and does not pay at once." How much more guilty is the one who does not pay at all.) The *Choshen Mishpat* (Chap. 97, Par. 4) rules it forbidden for a borrower to take a loan and squander it on needless things, to the extent that the lender will no longer find anything left from which to exact payment. One acting in this manner is called a *rasha'*. This is surely so where he has the means but refuses to pay the debt. How great is his iniquity!

One should also be aware that money retained illegally will not yield any gain in the long run, as Scripture puts it (Jer. 17.11): "He that gets riches and not by right; in the midst of his days he shall leave them." (*Ya'azvenu*, "he/it shall leave it/him" is interpreted both ways: Sometimes the riches will abandon the person; sometimes the reverse will occur). His misdeed will also cause the loss of whatever he had from before, as is found in *Derech Eretz Zuta* (Chap. 3): "If you have seized what is not yours, what is yours will be taken away."

That one should guard himself against misappropriating the property of others is included in the Scriptural admonition (Micah 6.8): "It has been told to you, O man, what is good and what God requires of you, only to do justice . . ." All this is included in the laws of justice — that a person should guard against harming his neighbor. (See Chap. 1, where we have elaborated on this theme.) Whoever takes care to conduct himself justly brings the Divine deliverance of Israel nearer, as it is written (Isa. 56.1): "Keep justice and do righteousness, for My salvation is near to come and My favor to be revealed." (See what we have written in the brochure *Sefath Tamim*, Chaps. 3, 4, and 5.)

III

1

THE IMPORTANCE OF SHOWING HOSPITALITY TO GUESTS

Chazal have declared (Sukkah 49b): "In three respects is *gemiluth chesed* greater than charity. Charity can only be done with one's money but *gemiluth chesed* can be done with one's person and one's money. Charity can only be given to the poor; *gemiluth chesed* both to the rich and the poor. Charity can only be given to the living; but *gemiluth chesed* can be done to the living and the dead." In the first two parts of this book, we have confined our discussion to the *chesed* performed with one's money: the giving to the poor and the extending of free loans to rich and poor. In this part we shall, please God, deal with the *chesed* extended with one's person.

Know that the concept of doing *chesed* with one's person includes all forms of kindness shown to his neighbor, exerting himself on the other's behalf. This includes hospitality to guests (here the mitzvah would be his endeavor to receive them graciously — even if they did not need his favors), visiting the sick, bringing joy to groom and bride, joining the funeral procession, burying the dead, eulogising him, carrying the bier, and many other acts which we shall, please God, enumerate further on.

First we shall elaborate on the greatness of the mitzvah of extending hospitality to guests, and the great reward which follows in its wake. Afterwards we shall describe how the mitzvah is to be performed. How precious is this mitzvah to God, may He be blessed! A whole section of the Torah is allotted to it. This fact indicates to us

189

that we are to observe the mitzvah devotedly all our lives. We find, too, that immediately after the episode of the visiting angels, Scripture praised Abraham since he would train his children also to follow in his righteous path.

The *Gemara* remarks (Shabbath 127a): "R. Yochanan said: Hospitality to guests is as great as early attendance in the Beth Hamidrash, and R. Dimi of Nehardea said: Even greater . . . (Cf. ibid.). The *Gemara* further declares that hospitality to guests is greater than welcoming the Divine Presence, as it says (Gen. 18.3): "O my Lord, if I have found favor in Your eyes, do not go away from Your servant." (He excused himself, asking the Shechinah to wait and not to leave till he returned; then he went to receive his guests.) This is also one of those deeds, the fruits of which are eaten in this world, while the stock remains for the world to come. So, too, the rest of the benefits which man receives through the exercise of *chesed* are bestowed for this mitzvah, since it too is included in the category of *chesed,* as the *Gemara* points out.

Now God, Who is great in counsel and mighty in deed, arranged that the marriage of Isaac to Rebecca should result from her approaching a traveller, as it is written (Gen. 24.14): "And it shall be the girl to whom I shall say: Let down your pitcher, I pray you, that I may drink, and she shall say: Drink and I will also give your camels to drink. She shall be the one that You have appointed for Your servant Isaac." As Rashi commented, "She is worthy of him, since she acts charitably." We can see from this incident, how high a person can reach through performing this mitzvah properly with a willing heart, like Rebecca, who in many respects did more than the servant requested.

If one performs this mitzvah continually, he is blessed, on that account, with sons. So the Midrash (Tanchumah, *Ki Thetzeh*) states, and so Scripture intimates by the episode involving Abraham. After the meal, the angel announced: "I shall surely return to you when the season comes around, and lo, your wife Sarah will have a son."

Know, too, that the mitzvah also includes the extending of hospitality to the rich. This is pointed out by the *Sefer Yesh Nochalin* quoting the *Maharil*. Even though the affluent have no need of favors, nevertheless the effort to serve and to honor them, as befits their dignity, constitutes a mitzvah. How much more is this so when the guests are poor! The mitzvah then becomes twofold, since the giving of charity is also accomplished, as is shown in the above-mentioned work (q.v.). Yet, our many sins have caused the practice to be reversed. When a rich friend pays a visit, the host shows him all manner of honor, and the reception is pleasant and gracious. When a sad and depressed person pays the visit, and the host should now fulfill the precept (Isa. 58.10): "And if you draw out your soul to the hungry and satisfy the afflicted soul, then shall your light rise in the darkness . . .", he is not too happy, and often even vexed.

On the authority of the *Mordechai,* the *Shach* (Yoreh Deah Chap. 256 Sub-sec. 1) rules that the members of a community may compel one another to house wayfarers and to deal charitably with them. The food eaten by the poor at one's table is considered a sacrifice burnt on the altar according to the *Gemara* (Chagigah 27a): "R. Yochanan and Resh Lakish both said: When the Temple stood, sacrifices would secure atonement for an individual. Now his table does." According to *Massecheth Derech Eretz* (Chap. 2), the merciful, who feed the hungry, give drink to the thirsty, clothe the naked and distribute charity are referred to in the Scriptural verse (Isa. 3.10): "Say of the righteous that it will be well with him, for they shall eat the fruit of their doings." The reward is all the greater if one invites a *Talmid Chacham* into his house. The *Gemara* (Berachoth 10b) teaches this lesson: "R. Yose b. Chanina in the name of R. Eliezer b. Yaakov: Whoever is host to a *Talmid Chacham,* feeds him, gives him drink, and grants him the use of his possessions, is regarded by Scripture as if he had sacrificed the daily (*tamid*) burnt offering. The word *tamid* appears here and also there (concerning the Shunamite who extended hospitality to Elisha):"He passes by us always" (*tamid*). (The inference being drawn by *Gezerah Shavah* – Tr.) Whoever withholds the enjoyment of his possession from a *Talmid Chacham*, is liable, God forbid, to suffer severe punishment. This is stated in the *Gemara* (Sanhedrin 92a): "R. Eleazar said: He who refuses the use of his possessions to *Talmidei Chachamim* will never be blessed with success.

Chazal stated (Sanhedrin 103b): "Great is the morsel (the food given to wayfarers), which drives away the near and brings near the far, removes scrutiny from the wicked and causes the Shechinah to rest on prophets of Ba'al. Even to transgress it unintentionally is regarded as a deliberate sin. 'It drives away the near' refers to Ammon and Moab. (Being descended from Lot, Abraham's nephew, they were near to Israel. The Allpresent drove them away, forbade them to join the Jewish community (i.e. the male descended paternally from an Ammonite or Moabite proselyte may not marry a woman of legitimate Jewish birth–Tr.), since they refused to meet the children of Israel with bread and water, as is recorded in Scripture. 'It brings near the far' refers to Jethro. As R. Yochanan stated: In reward for saying, 'Call him that he may eat bread, his (Jethro's) children were found worthy to sit in the Hall of Hewn Stone (the seat of the Sanhedrin – Tr.) . . . 'It shields the wicked from scrutiny' – his conduct is not examined to find cause for punishment. This is deduced from Micah, who made an idol (Judges 17.3 ff.). As Rabbah b. Mari stated: I have heard why Micah was not counted among the four commoners who have no share in the world to come. This was because he made his bread available to wayfarers. 'It causes the Shechinah to rest on the prophets of Baal' – as it is said (1 Kings 13.20): 'and it came to pass that they were sitting.' (Iddo, the prophet, had foretold that the altar in Bethel would be destroyed because Jeroboam had set up calves as idols there. A false prophet deceived him and persuaded him to return to Bethel, causing him to transgress the Divine command, 'You shall not return to Bethel.' This false prophet fed him. For that act the Shechinah rested on him and he prophesied, as it is written (Ibid.): 'And the word of God came to the prophet that brought him back'.) 'Even to transgress it unintentionally is regarded as a deliberate sin' — as R. Yehudah said in the name of Rav: 'Had Jonathan given two loaves of bread to David (the latter would not have had to ask for bread from the priests of Nov, Doeg would not have betrayed them to Saul), the priests of Nov would not have been slaughtered, Doeg would not have lost his share in the world to come, and Saul and his three sons would not have been slain." All we have written proves how important it is for one never to shut his eyes against the mitzvah of *hachnasath orchim*, hospitality to guests. In reward, the Holy One, blessed be He, will deliver him and his children from all the trouble of the world.

2

HOW TO TREAT GUESTS

The Torah, as we have seen, has gone to considerable length and detail to describe Abraham's reception of his guests, treatment not accorded to any of the other aspects of the Torah which Abraham fulfilled. In the other instances the Torah only remarks very generally that Abraham fulfilled the entire Torah (Gen. 26.5): "Because Abraham hearkened to My voice and kept My charge, My commandments, My statutes and My teachings." Now the general admonition "And you shall walk in His ways," which means that we should show kindness and goodness to others, includes *hachnasath orchim*. Yet the Torah described our forefather's hospitality at length, so as to teach us by example how to treat guests. It would be appropriate, then, for us to select a few details from this portion of the Torah, which have relevance for us.

First the Torah relates that Abraham was still ill, suffering the effects of his compliance with the command to circumcise himself. Nevertheless he sat at the entrance of his tent in the heat of the day, waiting and watching for some traveller he might discern from afar, to bring him to his house. (Even though we are not accustomed to act in this way, we can at least learn from here that one should go after guests, receive them most cordially, as if some wealthy person, who might benefit us considerably, were paying us a visit.) Next the Torah relates how Abraham ordered that water be brought for the wayfarers to wash their feet, for the simple reason that often travellers' feet become caked with mud and dust. He provided them the means to cleanse themselves (and we too should provide wayfarers with washing facilities, in addition to food and drink). Then Abraham invited his guests to rest from their fatiguing journey under the refreshing shade of a tree, while he went to prepare them something to eat. (From here we learn that, before preparing food for such guests, we ask them to rest and refresh themselves from the fatigue of their travels.) Abraham also noticed that they were unwilling to remain there and trouble him. He therefore remarked: "And I will fetch a morsel of bread ... after that you will pass on." He implied that they should eat just to still their hunger, and they could proceed on their way immediately thereafter. In the end he prepared a full meal in their honor. This is the habit of the righteous: they say little and do much. He served the food most elaborately, and with the maximum of dispatch. Whatever was ready first, was served first. He himself waited on them through the meal. When it was over, he escorted them on their way. All these acts should be learned from Abraham, our forefather. If one is unable to perform all of them, he should at least do some. We should also follow his example in training our own children in the observance of this mitzvah, as Scripture relates: "And he gave it to the lad," to Ishmael, to train him to fulfill mitzvoth (Rashi).

The holy books have admonished that, when guests come, one should receive them cordially. One should immediately place food before them, since the visitor might be poor and hungry and ashamed to ask. When serving them, the host should be gracious, not irritable. Even if he is depressed by worries, he should hide his affairs from them. He should appear to have means, even if he is poor, and his conversation should comfort and revive them. He should not disclose his troubles to them, for he will break their spirit in this way, since they will think that he says this on their account. He may forfeit his reward by such behavior. While they are eating, he should appear to regret that he is not able to provide them with more, as it is said (Isa. 58.10): "And you draw out your *nefesh*" — your desire to do good — for the hungry", *nefesh* denoting desire (See Gen. 23.28).

On the verse (Isa. 58.7): "Is it not to deal your bread to the hungry?" the Zohar (*Vayakhel*) elaborates: "The host should slice bread for his guest to prevent the latter becoming ashamed and embarrassed. The host should certainly not look at him while he is eating, so as not to humiliate him." If the guest sleeps over, the host should give him the best bed available, since it is very important for the weary to rest comfortably. Sometimes, the host who provides his guest with the opportunity to rest comfortably does better by him than in giving him food and drink. He should say to himself: "If I were a guest in his house, I would surely want him to show me consideration — to give me food and drink and a respectable lodging," as R. Chiya remarked to his wife (Shabbath 151b): "There is a revolving wheel in the world."

It often happens that a person is unwilling to invite a guest for a meal, since he feels that he cannot treat the guest well enough. This argument would only be valid if there were someone else who would take the guest and honor him as he deserves. If there is no one else to take the guest, then it is better for this person to invite him and treat him as well as possible, rather than leave the guest without food.

After the guest has finished his meal, the host must accompany him on his way. *Chazal* have ascribed very great value to this mitzvah, declaring (Sotah 46b) that it carries reward without limit. They have also expounded the verse (Deut. 21.6): "Our hands have not shed this blood, neither have our eyes seen it," in this way: "Can it enter our minds that the elders of the Beth Din shed blood? — They mean to say 'We did not see him and dismiss him without food, and we did not leave him without an escort.'" *Chazal* have further asserted that if a person accompanies someone setting out on a journey a distance of four cubits, the traveller will come to no harm. Hence whoever fails to escort him is like one who sheds blood. The community may compel individuals to escort travellers, just as it may force individuals to contribute to charity. Especially is this important when the guest does not know the way, and there are many forks and crossroads ahead. Then it is a great mitzvah to accompany the traveller and show him the way, or at least to give him such precise directions that he makes no mistake.

The merit of one who escorts his neighbor and helps him not to lose his way is exceedingly great, since this is the ideal in carrying out the mitzvah of escorting travellers. The Gemara (Sotah 46b) demonstrates the value of this mitzvah by citing this incident (Jud. 1.24): "And the watchers saw a man come forth out of the city, and they said unto him: 'Show us we pray you the entrance to the city, and we will deal kindly with you.' And he showed them the entrance to the city, and they smote the city with the edge of the sword; but they let the man go free with all his family." Scripture further relates: "And the man went into the land of the Hittites and built a city and called its name Luz." The Baraitha teaches (Ibid.): "This is the city against which Sennacherib marched without uprooting it, against which Nebuchadnezzar marched without destroying it, through which the angel of death has no permission to pass. When the old residents become tired of life, they go outside its walls and die. From here we reason by *kal vachomer*: Now this Canaanite did not utter a word or walk a step (he merely pointed his finger), yet he gained deliverance for himself and his descendants to the end of all generations. Whoever, then, actually does walk with someone to escort him will all the more be rewarded."

Scripture (Gen. 21.33) relates that Abraham "planted a tamarisk tree in Beersheba." *Avoth de R. Nathan* (Chap. 7) adds that he built large mansions by the wayside and left provisions there for the sake of passersby (see Sotah 10a). How worthy would it be for man to learn this virtue from Abraham our forefather! Every person should arrange to have a guest room. When his guest leaves in the morning, he will, then, naturally fulfill the mitzvah of escorting him.

The letters of the word *eshel* (tamarisk tree) are initials: aleph stands for *achilah*, eating; shin for *shethiah*, drinking; lamed for *leviah*, escorting. Others have lamed for *linah*, lodging. *Chazal* have stated: "And if one is unable to fulfill the mitzvah of providing the guest with food and drink properly, is he therefore not to perform the mitzvah of providing lodging and escorting?"

Let each person look at himself. Sometimes he builds extra buildings in his yard. He does not require them for sleeping facilities, but for less vital uses, and he convinces himself that these are a necessity for one purpose or another. So how can he then refuse to provide quarters for the needs of his soul? Now, if people individually cannot afford the cost, certainly the community is obliged to provide a hostel for wayfarers, so that they should not have to sleep outside. The community must also take care to feed them, and must by no means allow them to depart, God forbid, without food. *Chazal* (Sotah 46b) have remarked in commenting on the verse (Deut. 20.7): "Our hands have not shed this blood," that it conveys: "He did not come to our hand and we let him go without food." *Chazal* have also declared that "had Jonathan given David two loaves of bread" . . . as we have explained in Chapter 1. It has now become the standard practice in Jewry to found a *Hachnasath Orchim* Society which devotes itself to the fulfillment of this mitzvah. Happy is the lot of these people!

3

THE MITZVAH OF VISITING THE SICK

Now we shall proceed to explain the mitzvah of *bikkur cholim* (visiting the sick), another aspect of *gemiluth chesed*. Man enjoys the fruits of these acts in this world while the stock remains for him in the world to come (Shabbat 127a).

Chazal have exhorted us most keenly to observe this mitzvah. They have declared (Sotah 14a): "What is the meaning of (Deut. 13.5): 'You shall walk after *Hashem*, your God'? Is it possible for a human being to walk after the Shechinah? Has it not been said (Ibid. 4.24): '*Hashem*, your God, is a devouring fire'? The meaning is that one should follow the Attributes of the Holy One, blessed be He. As He clothes the naked, for it is written (Gen. 3.21): 'And God made for Adam and for his wife coats of skin and clothed them,' so you clothe the naked. The Holy One, blessed be He, visited the sick, for it is written (Ibid. 18.1): 'And God appeared to him by the oaks of Mamre,' so you visit the sick. The Holy One, blessed be He, comforted the mourners, for it is written (Gen. 25.11): 'And it came to pass after the death of Abraham that God blessed Isaac his son,' so you comfort the mourners. The Holy One, blessed be He, buried the dead, for it is written (Deut. 34.6): 'And He buried him in the valley,' so you also bury the dead." *Chazal* (Bava Metzia 30b) have further expounded the verse (Exod. 18.20): "And you shall show them the way that they are to walk in it" as follows: "The way" indicates *gemiluth chesed*. (This includes all acts of kindness through which one person may benefit another, whether by his person or his property — the latter referring to loans of articles. A special mitzvah specifically covers the case of cash loans, viz.: "If you will lend money to My people," hence the first mentioned verse is not needed for that.) "That they are to walk" — indicates visiting the sick. "In it" — burying the dead. Now the Gemara asks: "Is *Bikkur Cholim* not included in *Gemiluth Chesed*?" (So why should this require a special Scriptural reference?) The answer is that the special reference is required for the case where the visitor is the same age as the patient, since the former then carries away one sixtieth of the latter's illness. Nevertheless he is to make the visit.

Now the mitzvah of visiting the sick has no fixed measure or limitation. The distinguished is required to visit the plain person. The mitzvah is to be performed even several times a day, unless this becomes burdensome to the patient (Yoreh Deah, Chap. 335). Relatives and close friends come as soon as he takes ill; casual acquaintances wait till the third day, so as not to spoil his chances of recovery. If the patient is seriously ill, all come to him without waiting (Ibid.). If he lies on the ground, the visitor is not allowed to sit on a bench, since the Shechinah stands at the head of the sick. If the patient is in bed, this is permissible (Ibid.). The Shulchan Aruch rules further that visits are not paid to a person suffering from an intestinal illness so as not to put the sufferer to shame; nor to those with eye or head ailments since speaking disturbs them. The same applies in all similar cases. Hence the visitor does not enter their room, but remains in the corridor and inquires whether the patient needs anything. He perceives their suffering and prays for God's mercy. One should not neglect to invoke Divine compassion on every sick person he visits. If one spent time with the sick, but forgot to pray for Divine compassion, he has not fulfilled the mitzvah completely. The sick should not be visited during the first three hours of the day, for then their condition seems somewhat improved; the visitor will not feel the urgency of praying for them. Nor should they be visited in the last three hours, for then their condition becomes worse, and the visitor will despair of their recovery. (The hours mentioned here are relative; each constitutes one-twelfth of the daytime. To take each hour to be sixty minutes would mean that the mitzvah could not possibly be fulfilled on any winter's day which has less than six hours of day-light.) Now if one is in a hurry to proceed on a journey and can only come at these times, it would be better for him to visit the patient then, than not to come at all, since his visit may result in some benefit, like tidying up the room, etc., as the Gemara has remarked in the case involving Rabbi Akiva.

One may pray for the sick in any language he wishes since he is addressing his words directly to the Shechinah which is at the side of the patient. When not in the patient's presence, however, he should use Hebrew only, since angels have to bear his prayers aloft and they understand no other language. His petition should include the patient among the rest of the sick of Israel. Thereby his prayers will be more acceptable. He should say: "May the Allpresent have mercy upon you among the sick ones of Israel." For Sabbath, the formula is : "It is Sabbath, and it is forbidden to cry out. But the cure will come speedily, and His mercies are many. Have a peaceful Sabbath." The Gemara (Nedarim 40a) further assures that "he who visits the sick will be delivered from the punishments of *Gehennom*," as it says (Ps. 41.2): "Happy is he that considers the poor, *Hashem* will deliver him in the day of evil." *Dal*, poor, indicates the sick, as it says: (2 Sam. 13.4): "Why . . . are you becoming more sick?" (*dal*). "Evil" (*ra'ah*) indicates *Gehennom*, as it says (Prov. 16.4): "God has made everything for His own purpose; even the wicked for the day of evil" *(Gehennom)*. He receives reward in this world, as is recorded at the end of the verse: "God will preserve him and keep him alive; he shall be happy in the land." "God will preserve him from evil" — from the evil inclination; "keep him alive" — from suffering physical pain; "Let him be happy in the land" — that all accord him respect . . . (Cf. ibid.).

On the other hand, how great is the sin of those who are lax in the performance of this mitzvah, as the Gemara (ibid.) relates: "One of R. Akiva's disciples fell sick and the Sages did not visit him. R. Akiva therefore entered the house himself, and because they (followed him), swept and sprinkled the ground before the sick, he recovered. 'My master,' said he, 'you have revived me.' Rabbi Akiva went out and declared: 'He who does not visit the sick is like a shedder of blood.' " For the visitors attend to the needs of the sick and may know of some remedy or medical attention which might hasten his cure.

Now people, because of our many sins, are lax in observing this mitzvah, especially when the sick person is poor. I don't know what justification they have. The obligation exists where the patient is rich — even more so, then, when he is poor. If the poor is not visited, his very life may be jeopardized. Usually he cannot afford the food he needs in his illness. He has no one to consult with concerning his condition. Sometimes he cannot even afford to call a doctor or to buy medicine. His sufferings are aggravated in the winter when the severe cold crushes his depressed spirit. His worries increase when he realizes that he has lain in bed for several days, and no one has opened his door to care for him or to revive him. All these factors weaken his resistance and reinforce his illness, and this might cause his death. How should we appraise this dreadful state of affairs? People have to confess and say: "Our hand has not shed this blood." *Chazal* have interpreted this verse to mean, "We did not let him go without food" — that this would have been considered like shedding blood, since this might possibly have contributed to his death. How much more direct is the case here! The person is already ill; no attention is paid to him, and so his death is hastened. Certainly this would be too great a sin to bear.

In this connection, we may quote a relevant passage in the Gemara (Kethuvoth 67b): "The one who shuts his eyes against charity is like one who worships idols." The evil inclination tempts man to divert attention from the sick — to stay away from his home,

not to keep him in mind. If the healthy person were to come to the
sick, then the healthy one would inevitably, to some extent, have to
care for the sick. Yet he does not realize that a life is involved in such
behavior. (See what I have written in the note on Part II, Chap. 17,
in the Hebrew edition.)

On the other hand, how great is the reward granted by God, may
He be blessed, to one who does visit the poor, sick man, who does
advise him how to act, and who encourages him not to abandon
hope. For see, *Chazal* have described the greatness of the reward
just for visiting – it is even greater for one who also, in the same act,
fulfills the mitzvah of *tzedakah* and of saving a life, and who also
reassures and encourages the patient with his conversation. He will
be blessed in many important respects by *Hashem,* may He be blessed, as *Chazal* have made clear (Bava Bathra 10a): "Whoever reassures the poor will receive eleven blessings."

Indeed in many communities the practice has now been adopted
of forming a *Bikkur Cholim* Society for the purpose of caring for
these unfortunate souls when they are ill, to see that they receive
proper medical attention, proper food and all other necessities. How
commendable would it be were this the universal practice, especially
since human life is often involved! Whoever shuts his eyes against
this duty transgresses (Lev. 19.16): "Neither shall you stand idly by
the blood of your neighbor." Happy is the man who sets his mind
and heart on the sufferings of these crushed people. Of him, is it said
(Ps. 41.2): "Happy is he that considers the poor; *Hashem* will deliver
him in the day of evil." The poor mentioned here are the sick, as
Chazal have explained. And the reference is even more appropriate
to the sick who are poor, and therefore doubly crushed.

The Shulchan Aruch further requires the visitors to tell the patient
to arrange his affairs, if he owes money to others for instance, or
others owe money to him, if he has articles deposited with others, or
others with him. He should not fear, he is told, that this means that
he is going to die. This is done only after he has lain sick for three

days, unless he is already desperately ill. The *Chochmath Adam* also
mentions that it was customary in certain communities, and especially in Berlin, that, on the third day of a person's illness, the *Bikkur
Cholim* officers or others would come to him and say: "You know
that this is routine procedure, so have no worry on this account.
Make your will as you see fit. State what you owe and what others
owe to you." They also enjoined him to confess his sins, since
whoever confesses is forgiven. Because this is standard procedure in
these communities, the patient suffers no anxiety in arranging his affairs. Hence the same practice should be adopted in all communities.
Where no such custom obtains, the patient is not addressed thus,
since he might be made to fear that he is going to die. Plain people
become afraid when told to confess. When, however, the visitors
realize that the patient is in critical condition (or his disease is held to
be fatal), they steer the discussion with him to the point where they
advise him to confess, but not to fear. "Many have confessed and
recovered," they say, "while many who have not confessed have
died. You may even recover as a result of having confessed.
Everyone who confesses earns a share in the world to come." If he
cannot pronounce the words, he should think of them in his mind. If
he does not know what to say, he is told to repeat: "May it be His
will that my death atone for all my sins." None of these matters are
mentioned while ignorant people or women and children are present,
since they might begin to weep and so break the spirit of the patient.
He is also advised to ask the forgiveness of all against whom he
sinned either in money matters or by word of mouth. The reason for
this is that death does not atone for such transgressions, and his soul
might have to return to this world once more to restore the property
to its rightful owner, as the Vilna Gaon has noted in his comment on
(Prov. 14.25): "A true witness delivers souls." (Vid. ibid.)

In his notes, the author of the *Yesh Nochalin* quotes the words of
the Zohar (*Pekudei*): "Whoever watches over the sick, and tries to
make him repent, is a good angel. He causes the person to be

delivered from the attribute of strict justice, saves him from death, redeems him from the grave, and preserves his life. Of this one it is said: 'Happy is he that considers the poor.' " The righteous of speech will know how to reassure the sick, how to encourage him, comfort him, and set his mind at ease. The visitor should say: "For the merit of your repentance and confession, may you live; and if you should die, you will be cleansed of all your sins, you will be purified before God, receive your share in the world to come, have the merit of taking your place in *Gan Eden* among the *tzaddikim*." There (q.v.) too, this type of *chesed* extended to the sick by the visitor is elaborated, for when the latter encourages the former to repent, how great is his reward. So the *Zohar Chadash* puts it (Lech Lecha): "R. Abahu said: Come and see how great is the reward of the one who causes another to repent . . ." If the sick person has means, but has not met his charity and *chesed* obligations during his lifetime, he should be reminded to make amends, or at least to resolve, without binding himself by a vow, to attend to these obligations when he recovers. We have indeed found the writings of *Chazal* mentioning, several times, that charity delivers from death and from *Gehennom*.

4

TO ARRANGE ONE'S AFFAIRS
WHILE HIS FACULTIES STILL FUNCTION

Scripture admonishes (Eccl. 9.9): "Enjoy life with the wife you love all the days of the life of your vanity, which He has given you under the sun . . . for that is your portion in life." Next Scripture enjoins (Ibid. 10): "Whatever your hand obtains to do by your strength, that do; for there is no work, or reckoning (*cheshbon*), or knowledge (*da'ath*), or wisdom (*chochmah*) in the grave whither you go." We shall explain the sequence in this series by a story. There was once a very rich person, wise in all disciplines. One day he became poor. His condition grew worse, until he was not even able to provide his daily meals. He thought to himself: "I shall go abroad in the land. Perhaps, among the rich, I might find some position fitting my capabilities and knowledge. I shall certainly earn sufficient to maintain my standard of living." Now when he came to other localities and made inquiries whether a person of his caliber was needed, he was turned down. This continued for several days. By that time he had spent all the money he had taken with him. He saw that he could continue no longer. He therefore decided that it was wrong of him to seek such high office when his need was so pressing. So 'he looked for a lower position and found one. He earned a small salary, but was satisfied. One day, one of his former acquaintances met him. The acquaintance asked him how he was and what he was doing. He told the acquaintance how he had acquired his present position. The acquaintance said to him: "With your abilities, you should hold a much higher position." He replied: "I, too, would want it so. I looked about for many days. It then became a matter of life or death. I know what my situation would be, were I to return home. I would not even earn this amount. In my present depressed state, even this minor position, which God has granted me, is good enough for me. It at least gives me a living." This parallels our case. A person has to attend to three weighty and important matters while he is still in this world. Here they are, in descending order of importance: First, the study of Torah, which is the greatest of all. It earns greater reward than any other mitzvah, and the punishment for neglecting it is more severe than for any other transgression, The second is repentance, which is also most precious to, and beloved by, God. Third, the pursuit after mitzvoth and good deeds. This last is also of great importance, as it says (Prov. 21.21): "He that follows after righteousness and mercy finds life, prosperity and honor."

One more preliminary remark must be made. It is necessary to know that wisdom and knowledge in Scripture refer, according to the holy books, to Torah, since it is the source of wisdom and knowledge. Reckoning (*cheshbon*) refers to repentance. (So *Chazal* have indicated [Bava Bathra 78b] in expounding the verse [Num.21.27]: "Come to Cheshbon.") Now the phrases follow like pearls on a string. First Scripture enjoins (Eccl. 9.9): "Enjoy life with the wife you love." This speaks of Torah, which is symbolized by "wife" as *Chazal* have indicated. "You love" teaches that one should study that part of the Torah which attracts him (Avodah Zarah 19a). "All the days of your vanity" — warns that one should not let a single day pass without studying the Torah, for this is supremely important. He should dedicate himself to Torah study and then he will automatically come to repentance and good deeds. Our prayers, too, have been constructed in this form: the blessing for repentance begins with a petition for Torah. Only afterwards comes "And bring us near, O our King, to Your service." Whoever withdraws himself from Torah, thereby removes himself from the service of God. Next

King Solomon enjoined: "Whatever your hand obtains to do by your strength, that do." This takes account of the fact that a person is sometimes extremely preoccupied. He is completely incapable of concentrating on Torah study, or of engaging in the introspection required for repentance. He might reflect that there is no point in him pursuing mitzvoth, since he is devoid of Torah and repentance, which come first. Hence this admonition follows, since he will find nothing in the place where he is destined to go, which is the grave — neither wisdom nor knowledge (Torah), nor reckoning (repentance—rendering an account of his deeds), nor doing (mitzvoth). Hence one should snatch whatever he can while he is still in this world.

Now we shall elucidate what Scripture means by "with your strength, do it." At first sight the words "with your strength" seem superfluous. But they convey a very important thought, that a person should perform his Torah study and good deeds with *his own* person and property. He should not trust that his sons will complete the remainder of his duties during their lives and thereby raise his level of achievement. His sons will certainly also be preoccupied with their own affairs. They will not have the time even to carry out their own obligations and will leave these over to *their* children. So the person's hopes will remain forever unfulfilled. (Who, in the earlier generations, was greater than Hillel? His sons were certainly superior, pious saints. Nevertheless he warned [Avoth 1.14]: "If I am not for myself, who is for me?" So what shall we, insignificant beings, say? We see with our own eyes how the succeeding generations deteriorate. Who can tell whether the coming generation will be wise or foolish?) Hence King Solomon advised, "With your own strength, that do" — that one should complete everything himself, while he is still in full possession of his strength and vigor.

King Solomon also intended to convey another valuable idea. Sometimes a person is self confident. He thinks that, at the end of his days, he will draw his will and instruct his surviving sons to donate sums for Torah education and other worthy causes. There are various defects in this plan. Firstly,who knows whether his mind will then still function clearly? For this too, one needs the merit of being able to communicate his wishes to his children, since people die, may Heaven protect us, sudden or unnatural deaths. Then, who knows whether his sons will carry out his wishes? For it often happens, may Heaven protect us, that the lust for money distracts one's mind from obeying the will of his Creator and also of his father. Hence, King Solomon warned that it is far better for a person to arrange all his affairs, and set aside some portion for his soul, while he is still in full possession of his faculties, for then he will be wise enough to prevent his wishes being frustrated.

It would be well for him to transfer the money during his lifetime, and to invest it where it will yield a return for Torah education or *gemiluth chesed*. Then he will attain the blessing given by *Chazal* (Berachoth 17a) to those they loved: "May you see your requirements fulfilled in your own days." He should also choose some reliable and trustworthy friends and entrust the execution of his instructions to them.

All that we have written is tersely summarized in the *Sefer Chassidim* (Chap. 716): "Listen to advice while yet alive. Accept admonition from others. I have seen many give instructions to their household while ill and the directives were never carried out. So it says (Prov. 19.20): 'That you be wise in your latter end.'" Now if one had failed to make his will while he was still in full possession of his faculties, but was making his wishes known when he was near death, he should at least take the precaution to state his instructions in the presence of witnesses. So it says in the *Sefer Chassidim* (ibid.): "When man's days draw near for him to die, he should give his instructions in the presence of witnesses, and not rely even on his own father, certainly not on his wife and children." The reason is that children argue: since the father is dead, he no longer needs his property. But this is false. He needs his property more than they do.

Through the proper use of his possessions, he can still be rescued from the attribute of strict justice.

The Midrash aptly illustrates this situation with a parable: "There was once a man who had three friends. He loved the first very much, the second somewhat less. The third, he neither loved nor esteemed. Once the king issued a summons for this man, and the royal officers hastened to bring him to the palace. The man was terribly afraid. He suspected that he had been slandered and that he would be put to death innocently. All he could think of was to call and ask his good and reliable friend, the one he loved most, to go with him and testify to his innocence before the king. He went to this friend and told him what had happened, but the friend refused to go with him, and paid no heed to him. He left and went to his second friend. This one agreed to accompany him on the way to protect him from untoward incidents, but refused to appear before the king. As soon as they would reach the royal palace, he would leave and go home. The man then went to his third friend, whom he esteemed not at all, and asked him to go with him before the king. This friend replied: 'Don't be afraid. I'll go with you; I'll come to the king and testify on your behalf, and you will be saved.' He went, spoke up for the man, and saved him from harm. The first, most beloved of all friends, is man's money. It leaves him on the day he dies and gives him nothing to take with him, as it says (Ps. 49.18): 'His wealth shall not descend after him.' The second friend represents his sons and relatives who accompany him to the grave, then take their leave and depart. The third friend, the one who testified on his behalf, is his repentance and good deeds. These accompany him and testify on his behalf, as it says (Isa. 58.8): 'And your righteousness shall go before you.' The king who issued the summons is the King of kings, the Holy One, blessed be He, from Whose judgment no man can escape except by Torah and *ma'asim tovim* (good deeds)."

I have stated that the holy Torah itself has propounded this idea in the *Sidrah* of *Nasso* (Num. 5.10): "And every man's holy things shall be his; whatsoever any man gives to the Priest, shall be his." This verse intimates that in the end nothing remains of all man's accomplishments, with the exception of the holy acts that he performed, personally, during his lifetime, such as: *Tefillin, Tzitzith* and the other mitzvoth. Every mitzvah he performs creates another defending angel and these will forever keep company with him. Not so the *yetzer harah* and all his physical powers which man cherishes most. They accompany him temporarily; when he is in distress, they depart from him. Furthermore they really detest man. They ascend and testify against him, seeking to forfeit his life. Even the members of his own family, who really love him, cannot stay with him forever. Each of them must return to his own home, after they have escorted him to the cemetery. He will not see them ever again, until the time of the revival of the dead. What then does he retain? — his holy acts. They accompany him; they are his true friends and counsel, defending him before the Lord of all things. This thought is conveyed by, "And every man's holy things shall be his." Hence man should acquire as many of these friends as he can, during his lifetime. He should be with them at all times, since they will stay with him forever.

The verse ends: "Whatsoever any man gives to the Priest shall be his." This too teaches a moral lesson. Of all the money he exerts himself to accumulate in his lifetime, man will retain nothing in the end. The only sums he will continue to enjoy will be the amounts he distributed as charity and *chesed*. So *Chazal* have pointed out (Bava Bathra 11a): "My forebears laid up stores below; I have laid up stores above." This, then, is the meaning of the passage, "Whatsoever he gives to the Priest shall be his." The donation really belongs to the donor. The reason that Scripture uses the term "Priest" is because Priests and Levites were the main recipients of charity in ancient times. So Scripture has indicated (Deut. 12.19): "Take heed to yourself that you forsake not the Levite as long as you live upon the land." They were in need of care, because all Israel possessed land, while they did not.

5

CHESED TO THE DEAD
AND COMFORT TO THE MOURNERS

Burying the dead, beside being a mitzvah of the Torah, as it says (Deut. 21.22): "You shall surely bury him," also belongs in the category of *gemiluth chesed*. It is an even higher form, a *chesed shel emeth*, since no reciprocity can be expected here. Taking out the dead for burial, carrying the bier, joining the funeral procession, delivering the eulogy, and everything else done for the dead, involve *gemiluth chesed*. The topics are explained in the Torah portions of *Chayei Sarah* and *Vayechi*.

Now see how important this is. *Chazal* have ruled (Mo'ed Katan 27b): "If someone in the city dies, all are forbidden to carry on their occupations." Now, if the deceased had relatives, the main duty of attending to his burial would devolve on them. Nevertheless the entire city is duty bound to participate in the funeral. Hence all were forbidden to carry on with their work. They would thereby endeavor to prepare whatever was necessary for the burial. (If the community has organized groups, each assigned its particular day for discharging these obligations, then those not on duty are free to continue with their occupations. Where the members of the *Chevra Kadisha* have not been assigned specific days, but the entire society attends to the deceased, then they must all refrain from their regular occupations until their task has been completed and the coffin transferred to the pallbearers.) Even if the deceased had studied neither Tanach nor Mishnah, the rule applies: all work is prohibited. Torah study alone is not interrupted, as long as the funeral procession has not started, even if the deceased had studied Tanach and Mishnah. Once the coffin is taken out for burial, however, Torah study is stopped for one who was learned, even if the funeral is large, unless the number participating exceeds 600,000. Taking away the Torah (when a *Talmid Chacham* dies, his Torah departs) requires the same attendance as the giving of the Torah, which occurred in the presence of 600,000 men. Even the outstanding Torah scholar of the generation is not exempt from this obligation.

The Gemara (Kethuvoth 17a) relates of R. Yehuda b. Ilai that he would interrupt his studies to go to the funeral of a deceased who had read Scripture and studied Mishnah in his lifetime, and especially of one who had taught others. For an ignorant person, however, one is not obliged to interrupt his Torah studies, as long as others participate in the funeral and attend to the burial, the minimum being ten adult males for kaddish and the blessings of the mourners (Shulchan Aruch, Yoreh Deah, Chap. 361). I am indeed shocked at the laxity prevailing in some communities. As soon as a person escorts the bier a small distance and so fulfills this mitzvah, he returns home. The dead is deserted. Only a few individuals accompany him to the cemetery. Neither kaddish nor the blessings of the mourners can be recited. Surely it is incumbent on all the inhabitants of the city to see that a minyan is present until after the burial is completed, even though this sometimes entails much strain, for instance, in the winter season or where the cemetery is some distance from the city, in which case lots should be drawn to determine who should go. All that we have said applies to the burial of a person known not to have studied or to have achieved scholarship. Certainly our remarks apply with even greater force in our times when there is hardly a person who does not have some knowledge of Tanach or Mishnah (as is explained in the *Shulchan Aruch*). Obviously, then, this duty must be accorded the most careful attention.

The *Chevra Kadisha* must make every effort (once the government burial permit has been issued) not to be guilty of holding the dead unburied overnight. Great suffering is experienced by the dead if they are left unburied overnight as explained in the Zohar. The Torah prohibits this practice if they are held over for no reason, except in those cases permitted by the law (Vid. *Shulchan Aruch*). Many times, however, for some trivial reason or other, or from sheer laziness, as we have seen, the attendants postpone the funeral to the next day. Such practices must categorically be avoided.

Now let us deal with the eulogy. This also belongs in the category of the *chesed* extended to the dead. As *Chazal* have said (Bava Bathra 100b): "The eulogy is to honor the dead." (So Rashi has commented — Sukkah 49b. q.v.). It is a great mitzvah to eulogize the dead as befits them, to lift one's voice, to move those present to grief and weeping for the worthy person who has departed. *Chazal* have already remarked (Moed Katan 25a): "Whoever sheds tears for a worthy man obtains forgiveness for all his sins" and again (Shabbath 105b): "If one sheds tears for a worthy man, the Holy One, blessed be He, counts them and lays them up in His treasure house." Such behavior demonstrates that the mourner grieves sincerely at the resulting decrease in the service of God in the world. Every tear, then, is important in the eyes of God. Whoever is lax in lamenting a *Talmid Chacham* will, God forbid, suffer punishment. *Chazal* have declared that his days will not be prolonged; he deserves to be buried before his time. This matter should therefore be taken into careful account.

Now let us devote some attention to the topic of comforting the mourners. This too belongs in the category of *chesed*, as the Rambam has laid down (Laws of Mourning, Chap. 4). I subsequently found the *Pirkei de R. Eliezer* (Chap. 15) explicitly mentioning that comforting the mourners is an act of *chesed*. The Scriptural source is also indicated (Deut. 13.5): "After *Hashem*, your God, you shall walk." We have quoted this passage in full in Chapter 3. In addition, we have also found this virtue many times exemplified by Jacob and

David, etc., in the Torah and Prophetic Books. It is also included in the injunction (Lev. 19.18): "You shall love your neighbor as yourself." Whatever you wish others to do for you (whether helping you with what you need in your affairs, or lightening the burden of your cares when you are distressed) you should do for your neighbor. Therefore one must act accordingly whenever there are mourners, may God protect us. (Yet, because of our many sins, many treat this mitzvah lightly. Especially when poor people are in mourning, no one opens their door. But the contrary is true. The grief and loss of the poor are all the harder to bear, since these unfortunates derive pleasure from nothing else except their children. This line of reasoning appears in the Gemara (see Moed Katan 24b, in respect to the eulogy). I have noticed that this neglect is the result of the poor person having no friends and acquaintances in this world. Scripture has remarked (Prov. 19.4): "Wealth added many friends; but as for the poor, his friend separates himself from him." Indeed, his friend may be separated from him, but he is all the nearer to God. So Scripture has stated (Prov. 34.19): "God is near to them that are of a broken heart." How great is the recompense of those who comfort and speak encouragingly to them). The basic intent of *Nichum Avelim* is to give comfort to the mourners. One may fulfill his obligation by merely reciting: "May the Allpresent comfort you..." Nevertheless it is more desirable to speak comfortingly to them and to assuage their grief by some well-chosen remark, for this is the essence of *nichum*, comfort. See what we have written, further on, in Chapter 7, on a similar subject.

6

RABBINIC COMMENT ON GLADDENING GROOM AND BRIDE AND WHEN THE OBLIGATION IS NULLIFIED

To gladden the groom and bride is also an important duty, as *Chazal* have indicated on many occasions. It is also one of the forms of *gemiluth chesed*, as we see from *Pirkei de R. Eliezer* (Chap. 16). We have also learned this from the episode concerning the wicked Jezebel, the wife of Ahab. She was the one who incited him to worship idols and to shed the blood of Naboth of Jezreel. According to Scripture, her punishment was that dogs devoured her flesh. When her remains were collected for burial, only her skull and heels could be found. *Chazal* have explained that these limbs were left intact because her feet would dance and her head nod in honor of brides. Hence these were left over by the dogs. These facts demonstrate the greatness of the mitzvah.

Yet it is imperative not to cause more harm than good by this mitzvah. For instance, in many places, boys lacking in moral restraint and manners dance with girls, a culpable offence. Many prohibitions are transgressed in such acts. Or else, because of our many sins, other types of immodesty are indulged in. Such behavior occurs at weddings not conducted in the spirit of the Torah. One should flee from those places, since temptation is rife there. It is no mitzvah whatever to give joy to people who flagrantly disregard the word of God. Had the bride and groom raised an objection, these infractions would not have occurred. By remaining at such affairs, one causes much harm. On the other hand, if a person believes that, if he is present, the guests will listen to his admonition and will refrain from unseemly conduct, it is certainly a great mitzvah for him to attend and prevent transgression. The merit of causing the many to be righteous will be attributed to him.

The mitzvah of gladdening groom and bride reaches its highest form where not many guests are present, or when poor couples, or the children of parents who have become bereft of their wealth, marry. Few come to give them joy. At such weddings the word of God is not in any way transgressed. If some unseemly behavior does occur and attention is drawn to it, all will listen. It is a very great mitzvah to go to such weddings and bring joy to the couples. *Chazal* have said (Berachoth 6b): "Whoever gladdens the bridegroom is privileged to acquire Torah, and is considered as if he had sacrificed a thanksgiving offering in the Temple or as if he had rebuilt one of the ruins of Jerusalem." We have also seen how the most outstanding among *Chazal* conducted themselves on such occasions (see Kethuvoth 17a).

So far we have covered the mitzvah of the *chesed* extended by one's person — the mitzvah he fulfills by bringing joy. We shall now discuss the charity aspect, the *tzedakah* and *chesed* of contributing financially. This applies where, for instance, the families cannot afford the wedding costs or other such necessary matters. If one contributes or extends a loan — or, if he is unable to contribute his own money, but approaches others for assistance — how great is his reward! Note what the *Shulchan Aruch* rules (Yoreh Deah, Chap. 356, Par. 15): "Charity treasurers who have funds on hand should allocate them for the dowering of brides, since there is no greater charity." The *Chochmath Adam*, too, lays down (Chapter 154) that to provide for poor girls to marry, and especially orphans, is better than to give ordinary charity. (Firstly, the mitzvah of charity giving is fulfilled, and secondly, the great shame of the unmarried woman [Kethuvoth 67b] is removed. Furthermore, the world was not created to become void, but to be populated. Sometimes the woman might, God forbid, come to some harm.)

Several communities have adopted the custom of organizing a *Hachnasath Kallah* Society for helping orphans, or even those who have parents but are poor, to marry. Now, beside this important activity of making it possible for such girls to marry, and guarding them from evil, a great *chesed* is done to the parents. They weep and worry day and night once their daughters reach marriageable age and they are unable to help them. *Hashem*, to Whom all rewards belong, will surely recompense for all the good emanating from such acts, as we have explained above (Part II, Chap. 6).

7

"HAPPY IS HE THAT CONSIDERS THE POOR..."

This work of ours sets forth in detail the ways in which *chesed* is to be performed. The same topic is covered by the Scriptural passage (Ps. 41.2): "Happy is he that considers the poor *(dal)*..." Consequently I have decided to expound this passage to the best of the ability God has granted me.

The Psalm begins, "Happy is he that considers the poor; *Hashem* will deliver him in the day of evil." Now "wisely considering the poor" has many aspects, and the term poor has many ramifications, one of which is poor in money. If a person is financially poor, he often lacks all basic necessities: food, clothing, housing. So one has to consider the poor in all these three matters — that he should not lack food, as Scripture puts it (Isa. 58.10): "And you draw out your soul to the hungry"; that he be given clothes (Ibid.7): "When you see the naked, that you cover him"; that a house be rented for him *(Shulchan Aruch, Yoreh Deah,* Laws of Charity). If he is a wayfarer, lodging must be found for him, since Scripture ordains (Job. 31.32): "The stranger must not lodge in the street." The Gemara adds (Shabbath 118a): "If he stays overnight, he is given the means of lodging... a bed and pillow." These are the three basic necessities that have to be provided for the financially poor.

The keenest intelligence must be used in extending help to the poor person so that he will enjoy the maximum benefit and have to expend the least effort. Suppose, for instance, one lends or donates money to the poor. He should give it when the money can be used to the greatest advantage, when prices are lowest. A gift to a poor person should be given in a manner which allows the recipient to enjoy it without delay. For instance, when one gives clothes, the garments should be ready to wear. When food is given, it should be prepared, and the donor should take the trouble of bringing it to the recipient's home. Our conclusions are derived from the Talmudic dictum (Sukkah 49b): "The reward for charity is commensurate with the *chesed* in it, for it is said (Hos. 9.12): 'Sow for yourselves according to charity but reap according to *chesed.*' " Rashi elucidates: "The gift is the *tzedakah*: the effort in making the gift is the *chesed.* The donor puts his mind to benefit the poor, so that the money should not go to waste. He gives when grain is abundant; he takes the trouble to go to the poor man's home to give him food, ready to eat, and clothes, ready to wear." If a person is wise enough to give so that the recipient is unaware of his identity, as in the case of Mar Ukva, then happy is his lot. At the very least, one should guard the privacy of such giving, so as not to put the recipient to shame.

Giving intelligently involves, above all, observing how best to benefit the recipient, giving so as to extricate him from his poverty by granting a gift or loan, or by finding him employment, or any other means that will make him self-supporting. The donor fulfills the mitzvah of (Lev. 25.35): "And his means fail with you, then you shall uphold him." It is similarly stated in the *Sefer Chassidim*: "There is a form of giving which does not appear to be charity. Yet it has always appeared eminently so in the eyes of God. Suppose a poor man was selling some product or book which no one wanted to buy, and this person bought it from him. Or else the poor man looked for a position; no one wanted to hire him — but this man gave him employment. There is no higher form of *tzedakah.*" I have known rich and respected people of this type. They have undertaken certain business activities for the specific pupose of providing employment for poor Jews to earn a living. All this, and the like, is *tzedakah*, if not higher. Happy is their lot. We have dealt with the mitzvah of "and you shall uphold him" at length, above (Chap. 21, Cf. ibid.).

We have also encountered the term, *dal* — poor, referring to the physically weak, the sick. So Scripture describes him (2 Sam. 13.4): "Why, O son of the king, are you becoming more ill (*dal*) every day?" To deal intelligently with the sick requires, as *Chazal* have shown, to visit him, to observe whether it is possible in any way to hasten his recovery. We have previously explained what has to be done (Chaps. 3 and 4 — Cf. ibid.). This consideration must also be extended to the person who suffers persecution. One must try to devise some plan to extricate him from this distress.

There is another type of *dal*, the poor in intelligence, and his lot is the worst of all. *Chazal* have declared (Nedarim 41a): "No one is poor except the one who lacks wisdom." Here there are many classes. A person has foolish ideas, has strayed from the true path and become wicked. In this case, one has to think of ways to make him repent, how to restore him to the correct path. The merit for such an act is extremely great. The *Zohar Chadash* expresses it in these words (Lech Lecha): "R. Eliezer said: How great is the reward of a person who causes another to repent" (Cf. Ibid.). Others have no practical sense. They ruin their businesses. Sometimes such a person is exposed to public ridicule for his folly. Here, too, it is a mitzvah to open his eyes — to teach him, so that he should avoid ruining himself or suffering humiliation in the future. Suppose your son had gone to another city. How much would you desire that some upright and good individual provide your son with the knowledge and understanding to conduct his affairs! So you should act towards your neighbor. All this behavior is included in "And you shall love your neighbor as yourself." So the Rambam has laid down in his Code (Laws of Moral Dispositions, Chap. 10, Par. 3) in elucidating this mitzvah. One should take as much care of another's money as of his own. And he should desire his friend to be respected as much as he desires to be respected himself.

Then there is the poor in intelligence, in the simplest sense — the person who has no Torah education. The more fortunate person should consider ways to attract him to the Torah. This is certainly of paramount importance. As the Talmud puts it (Bava Metzia 85a): "R. Shmuel b. Nachmani said in the name of R. Yonathan: Whoever teaches his friend's son Torah becomes worthy of sitting in the heavenly Academy." *Chazal* stated further (Sanhedrin 99b): "Resh Lakish said: Whoever teaches his friend's son Torah is regarded by Scripture as if he created him . . ." On the Mishnaic dictum (Avoth 1.12): "Love people and bring them near to Torah", *Avoth de R. Nathan* has this to say (Chap. 12): "One should bend men and lead them under the wings of the Shechinah in the way that Abraham our father used to make men bend, and then lead them under the wings of the Shechinah . . . as it says (Gen. 12.5): 'And the souls that they had made in Haran.' "

One should be aroused to the same degree of compassion for such people as if he had seen someone naked without anything to wear. Indeed how shall that unfortunate clothe his soul in the upper world, if he is so bare of Torah and Mitzvoth? As it is known, Torah observance creates ornaments for one's soul, and one thereby earns the merit of sitting in the presence of God in His holy habitation. So it is written of Joshua the son of Jehozadak, the High Priest (Zech. 3.4): "Take the filthy garments from off him . . . and I will clothe you with robes . . . and they clothed him with garments." It is also recorded in the *Tanna debei Eliyahu Rabba* (Chap. 27):' "When you see the naked that you cover him' (Isa. 58.7) — How is this? — If you see a person devoid of Torah, take him into your house. Teach him *Shema* and *Tefillah*, and teach him one verse of Scripture or a single *halachah* each day. Stimulate him to perform mitzvoth. There is none more bare in Israel than he who has neither Torah nor mitzvoth. He is like a naked person." One also fulfills the commandment of "And you shall love Hashem your God," which also implies that you should make God beloved by His creatures, as *Chazal* have shown.

There is yet another, extremely important case in which consideration is to be shown to the poor. This occurs where the person does
not have the means to provide his children with a Torah education
and he is unable to teach them by himself. His children degenerate.
They remain utterly ignorant. Some even stray to evil ways. Hence it
is a great mitzvah to act wisely towards them, to provide them with
schooling. It happens that such children often succeed in their Torah
study, for the sake of their downtrodden fathers, as *Chazal* have
warned (Nedarim 81a): "Pay heed to the children of the poor, for
from them shall Torah go forth." The merit of a person occupied in
this way is very great, as the Gemara (Bava Metzia 85a) points out:
"If a person teaches Torah to the son of the ignorant then, even
though the Holy One, blessed be He, has issued an evil decree, He
rescinds it on that person's account."

There are many similar instances where one must be mindful of
the condition of the poor. I have, however, decided to be brief, since
the intelligent person can apply what has been said here to the other
instances. For the merit of such acts, *Hashem*, may He be blessed,
will deliver this person in the day of evil, as Scripture has promised.

8

CHESED BY WORD OF MOUTH:
THE MITZVAH OF SAVING ONE FROM DISTRESS

Chazal have pointed out that *chesed* can be done both with one's person and with his money. The *chesed* performed with one's person can be divided into three types: deeds, words, thoughts. So far, in the previous chapters, we have dealt mainly with such *chesed* as is performed in deed or thought —that is, to help one's fellow man by some effort or through some consideration — to devise a method or discover some advice to improve his condition, that he should not, God forbid, collapse. All this is included in the Scriptural admonition: "Happy is he that considers the poor."

Now we shall consider the *chesed* which man performs with his speech. A person may indeed incorporate this attribute in his words. First, in respect to Torah, the teaching of others is also a *chesed*. What he studies for himself is not *chesed*. As the Talmud declares (Sukkah 49b): "What does the expression mean (Prov. 31.26): 'She opens her mouth with wisdom and the Torah of *chesed* is on her tongue' — Is there a Torah of *chesed* and a Torah not of *chesed*? The Torah that is studied in order to teach is a Torah of *chesed*; the Torah that is not studied in order to teach is not a Torah of *chesed*." Next, suppose someone is angry at a person's friend. The person intercedes and so stills the man's anger. He is performing an act of *chesed*. It is written of Joseph (Gen. 40.14): "But have me in your remembrance when it shall be well with you and show kindness, I pray you, unto me and make mention of me to Pharoah and bring me out of this house." Furthermore, if one is able, by word of mouth, to prevent harm befalling another, this also constitutes *chesed*. An instance of this would be if, by chance, someone happened to meet a group of suspected robbers. He believed that they intended to rob someone, since he overheard them discussing this person's wealth. It is his moral duty to misrepresent, to say that the intended victim is poor, even though he knows, in his heart, that this is not true. All this is included in *chesed*. So we find Abraham telling Sarah (Gen. 20.13): "This is the kindness (*chesed*) which you shall show unto me: at every place . . . say of me: 'He is my brother.' " It would be even better if the person could forewarn the intended victim to guard himself against their nefarious designs. He is certainly obliged to do so, according to the law of the Torah (end of the Choshen Mishpat).

Again, if a person can convince someone to do a favor to a fellow man, this too falls in the category of *chesed*. The person will receive the blessing of *Hashem*, as we find in the Tosefta (Peah Chap. 3) — that even if one only as much as told others to give, reward is bestowed on him. So Scripture indicates (Deut. 15.10): "For because of this speech (read *davar* here as *dibbur*), *Hashem* your God will bless you . . ." See above (Part I Chap. 16) on the greatness of the reward for causing others to perform a mitzvah.

Thirdly, one can proffer good advice to a person in the conduct of his affairs, as is recorded in the *Choshen Mishpat* (Chap. 97 — Cf. ibid.), and this applies to rich as well as to poor people. Fourthly, if one finds a friend depressed by his poverty or some other trouble, and one is, God forbid, unable to help him, it is still a mitzvah to speak sympathetically to him to allay his anxieties. All these acts fall in the category of *chesed*. R. Yonah Gerundi has recorded in his *Iggereth Hateshuvah* that even if one is poor and cannot afford to engage in the concrete aspects of *gemiluth chesed*, nevertheless he can practise this virtue without money or cost. This is how such *chesed* is to be done: One should speak sympathetically to the poor and give satisfaction to the needy by his words, comfort them in the difficulties of their work and toil, and show them respect. *Chazal* (Bava Bathra 9a) have said that whoever gives a coin to the poor earns six blessings, while one who reassures with his speech earns eleven, as it says (Isa. 58.10): "And if you draw out your soul to the hungry and satisfy the afflicted soul; then shall your light rise in darkness and your gloom be as noonday. God will guide you continually and satisfy your soul in drought." Here the virtue is practised by speaking soothing words, by showing good will sincerely and graciously. Do you not see the explicit assertion that the reward for this act is very much greater than for giving charity, and the blessings are more numerous and significant? How great is this mitzvah! On its account, one is given life in the world to come, as we find (Ta'anith) in the incident involving R. Berokah. R. Yonah has also added that a person should submit suggestions to the community for improving the *tzedakah* and *chesed* activities. One receives special reward for initiating communal charity endeavors, in recompense for the souls he preserved. He himself will be the proof of the reward given for the charity he did. So Scripture states (Isa. 32.8): "But the generous devises generous things." And *Chazal* have declared (Bava Bathra 10a): "Greater is he who causes others to act, than he who acts alone." This is the real *ahavath chesed*.

There are many other types of *chesed* performed by word of mouth, for instance to pray that God heal the sick. This is included in visiting the sick (*bikkur cholim*), which is also a *gemiluth chesed*. So we find in the Gemara and in the *Yoreh Deah* (Chap. 335). We have already quoted the paragraph (see Chapter 3 above). The same applies to the harm that threatens a person even without his knowing about it. We found that Abraham interceded on behalf of the men of Sodom in such an instance. He pleaded that they be spared. How much more does this apply when a fellow Jew is involved!

Whoever studies the first eight chapters, and these subsequent thirty-two, will see that the mitzvah of *chesed* is involved in all the good that there is in the world. Every person can exercise this virtue in his affairs, and sometimes even by mere, simple acts, where the recipient benefits while the donor loses nothing. Yet people make light of this, because of our many sins. So I believe that the Midrash quoted by the *Sefer, Lev David*, would be appropriate to our discussion. "Elijah, of blessed memory, was walking with R. Yehoshua b. Levi. As they walked along, Elijah pointed to a large square where a crowd of people had congregated at one of the stores and were bargaining. They were jostling and pushing one another. Elijah and R. Yehoshua approached the store and discovered, in all the pushing, that the store was selling putrid dog's meat at a *dinar* per *litra*. Yet the customers kept pushing, each trying to get ahead of the other. The two proceeded on their way and came to another square. It was empty. A single store was selling prime veal at a *perutah* per *litra*. Yet there were no customers. R. Yehoshua was astounded. 'Don't be surprised at tastes,' Elijah told him. 'The store selling putrid meat is illustrative of the masses who expend their might and squander their money to pursue sin, which is like a decomposing dog. On the other hand, Torah and mitzvoth may be compared to prime meat, and are cheap to come by. Yet there are no customers.' "

So I say here. Sometimes it is easy for a person to lavish thousands of dollars on worthless trifles which the evil inclination foists on him as, for instance, to revel in and gloat over some victory or to achieve specious honor. People even expend enormous effort on something that brings them no benefit whatever, neither in this nor in the next world. Such activities are no better than dog's carcasses. As for *chesed*, here the good inclination acts as broker, announcing that its merchandise is legitimate and that God Himself trades in it (as it is written [Micah 7.18]: "For He delights in *chesed*"). It brings happiness to man in this world and the next. It is cheaply bought, and requires no effort. Yet, on account of our many sins, no one gives this lucrative business the attention it deserves. The reason for its neglect is that the *yetzer harah* does not let go of man. It does not let him see the greatness and goodness of the mitzvah of *chesed*.

The best advice to follow here is to ponder constantly over Scriptural verses and Rabbinic literature which heap praise on this holy virtue. Then one will gain the clear conviction that this is in truth God's will: that we should train ourselves to behave with kindness and mercy towards our fellow men, in the words of Scripture: "To walk in all His ways." The *Sifrei* declares (Deut. 11.22): "These are the ways of God: '*Hashem, Hashem*, merciful and gracious God, long-suffering and abundant in chesed . . .'" Following this line of conduct, one will come to love the virtue of *chesed*, as it is written: *Ahavath chesed* (to love kindness). And for the merit of such behavior, God will extend kindness to this person in all his affairs, both in this world and the next.

Nevertheless one should not delude himself and believe that it is enough to embody this virtue and neglect the fear of Heaven altogether, God forbid. This is false. One needs to follow and obey the Torah, to accept the yoke of Heaven, and to also pursue the ways of *chesed* energetically. The verse (Deut. 32.39): "If they were wise, they would understand this" is expounded by the *Sifrei*: "Had Israel studied the words of the Torah, no evil would have gained mastery over them. What did I say to them? — Accept the yoke of the Kingdom of Heaven, persuade each other to fear Heaven and behave towards each other in *chesed*." Then they will have peace and happiness.

EPILOGUE

Now I know that many people think that, in this day and age, the practice of charity and *chesed* has become sufficiently widespread, and nothing more need be said about it. To such an argument I would reply: Charity, as is well known, is measured relative to the giver and the receiver — as far as the recipient is concerned, according to his needs, since the Torah has ordained: "You shall surely open your hand to him and surely lend him sufficient for his need." In earlier times the needs of the poor could easily be satisfied by some small gift. Today clothing, shoes and housing and the other daily, basic necessities are much more expensive. One should look at his own self, his own expenditures, and he will see that, today, the costs of almost everything have doubled and quadrupled. Hence the obligation to satisfy the needs of the poor also requires much larger sums. The same applies to the *chesed* we have been commanded to do in making loans to the poor, as the Torah ordains: "If you will lend money to My people, to the poor with you." It is also written, "And if your brother grow poor and his means fail with you, then you shall uphold him." This matter is included as well, as has been explained above (Chap. 1). So too in earlier times a person needed little for his sustenance and a small loan was sufficient for him to engage in trade, to maintain himself and his family. The lender was thereby able to fulfill the injunction of the Torah to uphold the poor. This is not so today, when the needs are much greater. The margin of profit in every business transaction is smaller now, also. Hence every man needs much more to make a living.

229

Giving is also relative to the donor, since the obligation to give charity depends on each person's circumstances. The obligation of the well-to-do is much greater than that of the poor (the latter too must contribute to charity — see Gittin 7a). The obligation of the rich is greater than that of the well-to-do. As for the extremely wealthy person, his obligation is all the greater than that of the others. Now, two people may perform exactly the same act. The one is praiseworthy and receives reward. The other is condemned to lose his money. The reason is that, for the latter, the gift was trivial in comparison with the blessing God, may He be blessed, had bestowed on him. A case in point is the incident involving Nakdimon b. Gurion (Kethuvoth 67b). He was indeed a very prominent person. He was one of the three for the sake of whom the world enjoyed sunshine, as is related in the Gemara (Ta'anith 20a). He dispensed charity and *chesed* to all Israel (see Kethuvoth, Ta'anith ibid.). Nevertheless, because he had not contributed in accordance with his means, he was condemned to lose his fortune. Obviously we cannot evaluate today's obligations with the criteria of former times. Formerly, less wealth had been accumulated in the world. Today there are indeed enormously wealthy people, and many more affluent individuals than ever before. (Everyone can appraise the true state of affairs in his own city. One who was affluent by former standards is considered relatively poor today. Whoever was once considered wealthy is not even regarded as well-to-do today. By comparison with former times, there are also more poor people today, and the obligation of the rich to help, in the time of need, is therefore increased. So how can we regard the obligations to have remained the same as they were before?)

In former times people lived on very low standards. They only spent money for basic necessities. In time of emergency, it was sufficient to fulfill one's charity obligations with the modest sum of money one held ready for *tzedakah* and *chesed*. Circumstances have changed. People spend much of their money on luxuries and pleasures, on expensive clothes and homes, on domestic help and the like. The measure of man's charity and *chesed*, which involves his very life and soul, his deliverance in this world and the next, should not be less than for one of these luxuries. Our remarks are indicated in the assertion of *Chazal*: "God will in the future reprove each person in relation to what he is." Now, when we ask someone how he deals with his household expenses, behaving like a rich man, spending more than his means allow, he answers readily that he finds it impossible to reduce these expenditues by any amount. He trusts that God will, on that account, help him. Yet when a charity case is brought to his notice, he hardens his heart and closes his fist, giving the impression that he is poor and impoverished. He does not even contribute in accordance with his means. On this matter, Scripture has remarked (Prov. 13.7): "There is that pretends himself rich (in his own affairs), yet has nothing. There is that pretends himself poor (in giving charity and doing chesed), yet has great wealth."

As is known, charity and *chesed* overcome the attribute of strict justice. On the verse (Deut. 13.18): "And He will give you mercy and have compassion on you," *Chazal* have commented (Shabbath 151b): "Whosoever has mercy on human beings will be granted mercy from Heaven." In these times we see with our own eyes how the attribute of strict justice grows stronger in the world from day to day. All kinds of maladies and unnatural deaths abound. There is a lack of Divine influence in the world, so that each day is more cursed than the day before. How much must we increase the prevalence of *tzedakah* and *chesed*. Perhaps in this way, we shall succeed in averting the severity of the judgment and the world will become filled with mercy (as we have explained [Part II, Chap. 3, ibid.].)